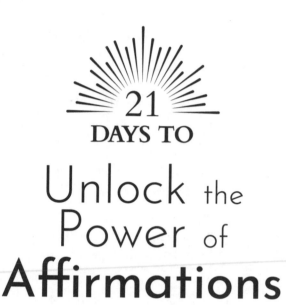

21
**DAYS TO**

Unlock the
Power of
**Affirmations**

# Also in the 21 Days series

*21 Days to Awaken the Writer Within*
by Lisa Fugard

*21 Days to Become a Money Magnet*
by Marie-Claire Carlyle

*21 Days to Decode Your Dreams*
by Leon Nacson

*21 Days to Explore Your Past Lives*
by Denise Linn

*21 Days to Find Success and Inner Peace*
by Dr. Wayne W. Dyer

*21 Days to Master Numerology*
by David A. Phillips

*21 Days to Understand Qabalah*
by David Wells

*21 Days to Work with Crystals*
by Judy Hall

# 21 DAYS TO

# Unlock the Power of Affirmations

## Manifest Confidence, Abundance, and Joy

# LOUISE HAY

**HAY HOUSE**

Carlsbad, California • New York City
London • Sydney • New Delhi

**Published in the United Kingdom by:**
Hay House UK Ltd, The Sixth Floor, Watson House,
54 Baker Street, London W1U 7BU
Tel: +44 (0)20 3927 7290; www.hayhouse.co.uk

**Published in the United States of America by:**
Hay House Inc., PO Box 5100, Carlsbad, CA 92018-5100
Tel: (1) 760 431 7695 or (800) 654 5126; www.hayhouse.com

**Published in Australia by:**
Hay House Australia Pty Ltd, 18/36 Ralph St, Alexandria NSW 2015
Tel: (61) 2 9669 4299; www.hayhouse.com.au

**Published in India by:**
Hay House Publishers India, Muskaan Complex,
Plot No.3, B-2, Vasant Kunj, New Delhi 110 070
Tel: (91) 11 4176 1620; www.hayhouse.co.in

A catalogue record for this book is available from the British Library.

Tradepaper ISBN: 978-1-4019-7121-2
E-book ISBN: 978-1-78817-893-8
Audiobook ISBN: 978-1-78817-850-1

10 9 8 7 6 5 4 3 2 1

Interior illustrations: Shutterstock

Printed in the United States of America

# Contents

# Publisher's Note

Research has shown that establishing a habit requires 21 days' practice. That's why Hay House has decided to adapt the work of some of its most prestigious authors into these short, 21-day courses, designed specifically to develop new mastery of subjects such as affirmations.

Other titles that will help you to explore further the concepts featured in the 21-day program are listed at the beginning of this book.

*21 Days to Unlock the Power of Affirmations* draws from Louise Hay's best-selling *Experience Your Good Now!* (Hay House, 2010), *I Can Do It*® (Hay House, 2004), and *You Can Heal Your Life* (Hay House, 1984, 2009).

# Author's Note

Many of the exercises in the chapters that follow need to be done on a separate piece of paper, so I recommend that you keep a pad of paper or a blank journal and a pen handy as you use this book.

# Introduction

Welcome to the world of affirmations. By choosing to use the tools in this book, you've made a conscious decision to heal your life and move forward on the path of positive change... and the time for that positive change is now! There is no time like the present for you to take control of your thoughts. Join the countless numbers of people who have changed their lives for the better by doing what I'm going to suggest to you in these pages.

Doing affirmations is not hard work. It can be a joyous experience as you lift the burden of old negative beliefs and release them back to the nothingness from whence they came.

Just because we've believed something negative about ourselves or about our lives does not mean that there is any truth to it. As children, we hear negative things about ourselves and about life and we accept these ideas as if they're true. Now, we're going to examine the things we've believed and make a decision to either continue to believe them because they support us and make our life joyful and fulfilled, or make the decision to release them. I like to imagine that I'm letting go of old beliefs by dropping them into a river, and they gently drift downstream and dissolve and disappear, never to return again.

Come into my garden of life and plant new thoughts and ideas that are beautiful and nourishing. Life loves you and wants you to have the very best. Life wants you to have peace of mind, inner joy, confidence, and an abundance of self-worth and self-love. You deserve to feel at ease at all times with all people and to earn a good living. So let me help you plant these ideas in your new garden. You can nourish them and watch them grow into beautiful flowers and fruits that will in turn feed and nourish you all of your life.

# DAY 1

# What Are Affirmations?

For those of you who aren't familiar with affirmations and have never worked with them, I'd like to explain a little about what they are and how they work. Very simply, an affirmation is anything you say or think. A lot of what people normally say and think is quite negative and doesn't create good experiences. You have to retrain your thinking and speaking into positive patterns if you want to heal your life.

An affirmation opens the door. It's a beginning point on the path to change. In essence, you're saying to your subconscious mind: "I am taking responsibility.

I am aware that there is something I can do to change." When I talk about doing affirmations, I mean consciously choosing words that will either help eliminate something from your life or help create something new in your life.

Every thought you think and every word you speak is an affirmation. All of your self-talk, your internal dialogue, is a stream of affirmations. You're using affirmations every moment whether you know it or not. You're affirming and creating your life experiences with every word and thought.

Your beliefs are merely habitual thinking patterns that you learned as a child. Many of them work very well for you. Other beliefs may be limiting your ability to create the very things you say you want. What you want and what you believe you deserve may be very different. You need to pay attention to your thoughts so that you can begin to eliminate the ones creating experiences you do not want in your life.

Please realize that every complaint is an affirmation of something you think you don't want in your life.

Every time you get angry, you're affirming that you want more anger in your life. Every time you feel like a victim, you're affirming that you want to continue to feel like a victim. If you feel that life isn't giving you what you want, then it's certain that you'll never have the goodies that life gives to others—that is, until you change the way you think and talk.

You're not a bad person for thinking the way you do. You've just never learned how to think and talk. People throughout the world are just now beginning to learn that thoughts create experiences. Your parents probably didn't know this, so they couldn't possibly teach it to you. They taught you how to look at life in the way that their parents taught them. So nobody is wrong. However, it's time for you to wake up and begin to consciously create your life in a way that pleases and supports you. You can do it. I can do it. We all can do it—we just need to learn how.

Throughout this book, I'll talk about specific topics and concerns, from self-esteem and fearful emotions to critical thinking and forgiveness; from health and aging to job success, money, and prosperity; and from loving yourself to friendship, love, and intimacy. I will also give you exercises that will show you how to make positive changes in these areas.

Some people say "affirmations don't work" (which is an affirmation in itself), when what they mean is that they don't know how to use them correctly. They may say, "My prosperity is growing," but then think, *Oh, this is stupid, I know it won't work.* Which affirmation do you think will win out? The negative one, of course, because it's part of a long-standing, habitual way of looking at life. Sometimes people will say their affirmations once a day and complain the rest of the time. It will take a long time for affirmations to work if they're done that way. The complaining affirmations will always win, because there are more of them, and they're usually said with great feeling.

However, saying affirmations is only part of the process. What you do the rest of the day and night is even more important. The secret to having your affirmations work quickly and consistently is to prepare an atmosphere in which they can grow. Affirmations are like seeds planted in soil. Poor soil, poor growth. Rich soil, abundant growth. The more you choose thoughts that make you feel good, the quicker the affirmations work.

So think happy thoughts. It's that simple. And it is doable. The way you choose to think, right now, is just that—a choice. You may not realize it because you've thought this way for so long, but it really is a choice.

Now... today... this moment... you can choose to change your thinking. Your life won't turn around overnight, but if you're consistent and make the choice on a daily basis to think thoughts that make you feel good, you'll definitely make positive changes in every area of your life.

# DAY 2

# The Power of Affirmations

Today is a new day. Today is a day for you to begin creating a joyous, fulfilling life. Today is the day to begin to release all your limitations. Today is the day for you to learn the secrets of life. You can change your life for the better. You already have the tools within you to do so. These tools are your thoughts and your beliefs. In this book, I will teach you how to use these tools to improve the quality of your life.

I wake up each morning with blessings and gratitude for the wonderful life I lead, and I make the choice to think happy thoughts no matter what others are doing. No, I don't do this 100 percent of the time, but I am up to about 75 or 80 percent right now, and it's made a big difference in how much I enjoy life and how much good just seems to flow into my everyday world.

The only moment you ever live in is this moment. It's the only time you have any control over. "Yesterday is history, tomorrow is a mystery, today is a gift, which is why we call it the present." My yoga teacher, Maureen MacGinnis, repeats this in every class she teaches. If you don't choose to feel good in this moment, then how can you create future moments that are abundant and fun?

How do you feel right now? Do you feel good? Do you feel bad? What are your current emotions? What is your gut feeling? Would you like to feel better? Then reach for a better feeling or thought. If you feel bad in any way—sad, grumpy, bitter, resentful, angry, fearful, guilty, depressed, jealous, critical, and so on—then you've temporarily lost your connection to the flow of good experiences that the Universe has waiting for you. Don't waste your thoughts on blame.

No person, place, or thing has any control over your feelings because they don't think in your mind.

This is also why you really have no control over others—you see, you can't control their thoughts. No one can control another unless that person gives permission. So you want to be aware of this powerful mind you have. You can take total control over your own thinking. It's the only thing you'll ever have total control of. What you choose to think is what you'll get in life. I've chosen to think thoughts of joy and appreciation, and you can, too.

What kinds of thoughts make you feel good? Thoughts of love, appreciation, gratitude, joyful childhood experiences? Thoughts in which you rejoice that you're alive and bless your body with love? Do you truly enjoy this present moment and get excited about tomorrow? Thinking these kinds of thoughts is an act of loving yourself, and loving yourself creates miracles in your life.

Doing affirmations is consciously choosing to think certain thoughts that will manifest positive results in the future. They create a focal point that will allow you to begin changing your thinking. Affirmative statements are going beyond the reality of the present into the creation of the future through the words you use in the now.

When you choose to say "I am very prosperous," you may actually have very little money in the bank at the moment, but what you're doing is planting seeds for future prosperity. Each time you repeat this statement, you're reaffirming the seeds you've planted in the atmosphere of your mind. That's why you want it to be a happy atmosphere. Things grow much quicker in fertile, rich soil.

It's important for you to always say your affirmations in the present tense, and without contractions. (Although I use contractions throughout the running text of my books, I never use them in affirmations, since I don't want to diminish their power.) For example, typical affirmations would start: "I have…" or "I am…" If you say, "I am going to…" or "I will have…" then your thought stays out there in the future. The Universe takes your thoughts and words very literally and gives you what you say you want. Always. This is another reason to maintain a happy mental atmosphere. It's easier to think in positive affirmations when you feel good.

Think of it this way: Every thought you think counts, so don't waste your precious thoughts. Every positive thought brings good into your life. Every negative thought pushes good away; it keeps it just out of your reach. How many times in your life have you almost gotten something good and it seemed to be snatched away at the last moment? If you could remember what your mental atmosphere was like at those times, you'd have the answer. Too many negative thoughts create a barrier against positive affirmations.

If you say, "I don't want to be sick anymore," this is not an affirmation for good health. You have to state clearly what you do want: "I accept perfect health now." "I hate this car" does not bring you a wonderful new car because you're not being clear. Even if you do get a new car, in a short time you'll probably hate it, because that's what you've been affirming. If you want a new car, then say something like this: "I have a beautiful new car that suits all of my needs."

You'll hear some people saying, "Life sucks!" (which is a terrible affirmation). Can you imagine what experiences that statement will attract to you? Of course, it isn't life that sucks, it's your thinking that sucks. That thought will help you feel terrible. And when you feel terrible, no good can come into your life.

Don't waste time arguing for your limitations: Poor relationships, problems, illnesses, poverty, and so on. The more you talk about the problem, the more you anchor it in place. Don't blame others for what is seemingly wrong in your life—that's just another waste of time. Remember, you're under the laws of your own consciousness, your own thoughts, and you attract specific experiences to you as a result of the way you think.

When you change your thinking process, then everything in your life will also change. You'll be amazed and delighted to see how people, places, things, and circumstances can change. Blame is just another negative affirmation, and you don't want to waste your precious thoughts on it. Instead, learn to turn your negative affirmations into positive ones. For instance:

| I hate my body. | *becomes* | I love and appreciate my body. |
|---|---|---|
| I never have enough money. | *becomes* | Money flows into my life in an abundant way. |
| I'm tired of being sick. | *becomes* | I allow my body to return to its natural, vibrant health. |
| I'm too fat. | *becomes* | I honor my body and take good care of it. |
| Nobody loves me. | *becomes* | I radiate love, and love fills my life. |
| I'm not creative. | *becomes* | I am discovering talents I did not know I had. |
| I'm stuck in a lousy job. | *becomes* | Wonderful new doors are opening for me all the time. |
| I'm not good enough. | *becomes* | I am in the process of positive change, and I deserve the best. |

This doesn't mean that you have to be worried about every thought you think. When you first begin to make the changeover and really pay attention to your thoughts, you'll be horrified to realize how negative much of your thinking has been. So when you catch a negative thought, just think to yourself: *That is an old thought; I no longer choose to think that way.* Then find a positive thought to replace it as quickly as you can. Remember, you want to feel good as much as possible. Thoughts of bitterness, resentment, blame, and guilt make you feel miserable. And that's a habit you really want to release.

Affirmations are solutions that will replace whatever problem you might have. Whenever you have a problem, repeat over and over:

*"All is well. Everything is working out for my highest good. Out of this situation only good will come. I am safe."*

This simple affirmation will work miracles in your life.

I would also suggest that you avoid sharing your affirmations with others who may pooh-pooh these ideas. When you're just getting started, it's best to keep your thinking to yourself until you've achieved your desired results. Then your friends will say, "Your life is changing so much. You're so different. What have you been doing?"

Go over this chapter several times until you really understand the principles and can live them. Also, zero in on the chapters that have the most meaning to you, and practice those particular affirmations. And remember to make up affirmations of your own.

Some affirmations you can use right now are:

*"I can feel good about myself!"*

*"I can make positive changes in my life!"*

*"I can do it!"*

# DAY 3

# Self-esteem

Today we're going to look at the topic of self-esteem. One thing is certain and that is you'll never have good self-esteem if you have negative thoughts about yourself. Self-esteem is merely feeling good about yourself, and when you do so, you develop confidence. Confidence then builds self-esteem—each step feeds upon the other. Once you get the rhythm going, you can accomplish almost anything.

Since self-esteem is what you think about yourself, you've the freedom to think anything you want. So why would you want to belittle yourself?

You were born extremely confident. You came into this world knowing how wonderful you are. You were so perfect when you were a tiny baby. You didn't have to do anything—you were already perfect—and you acted as if you were aware of that. You knew you were the center of the Universe. You weren't afraid to ask for what you wanted. You freely expressed your emotions. You mother knew when you were angry; in fact, the entire neighborhood knew it. And when you were happy, your smile lit up the whole room. You were so full of love and confidence.

Little babies will die if they don't get love. Once we're older, we learn to live without love, but no baby will stand for that. Babies also love every inch of their bodies, even their own feces. They have no guilt, no shame, no comparisons. They know they're unique and wonderful.

You were like that. Then somewhere during your childhood, your well-meaning parents passed on their own insecurities and taught you feelings of inadequacy and fear. At that point, you began to deny your own magnificence. These thoughts and feelings were never true, and they certainly aren't true now. So I want to bring you back to the time when you really knew how to be confident.

## Exercise: I Approve of Myself

I've given this exercise to hundreds of people, and the results are phenomenal. For the next month, say over and over to yourself, "I approve of myself."

Do this 300 or 400 times a day, at least. No, it's not too many times. When you're worrying, you go over your problem at least that many times. Let "I approve of myself" become a walking mantra, something you just say over and over and over to yourself, almost nonstop.

Saying "I approve of myself" is a guaranteed way to bring up everything buried in your consciousness that's in opposition.

When negative thoughts come up, such as, "How can I approve of myself when I am fat?" or "It's silly to think this can do any good," or "I am no good," or whatever your negative babble will be, this is the time to take mental control. Give these thoughts no importance. Just see them for what they are—another way to keep you stuck in the past. Gently say to these thoughts, "I let you go; I approve of myself."

Even considering doing this exercise can bring up a lot of stuff, like "It feels silly," "It doesn't feel true," "It's a lie," "It sounds stuck up," or "How can I approve of myself when I do that?"

Let all these thoughts just pass through. These are only resistance thoughts. They have no power over you unless you choose to believe them.

"I approve of myself, I approve of myself, I approve of myself." No matter what happens, no matter who says what to you, no matter who does what to you, just keep it going. In fact, when you can say that to yourself as someone is doing something you don't approve of, you will know you're growing and changing.

Thoughts have no power over us unless we give in to them. Thoughts are only words strung together. They have *no meaning whatsoever*. Only we give meaning to them. Let us choose to think thoughts that nourish and support us.

To look yourself in the eye and make a positive declaration is one of the quickest ways to get positive results with affirmations. I ask people to look in their eyes and say something positive about themselves every time they pass a mirror.

So choose new thoughts to think about yourself, and choose new words to tell yourself how magnificent you are and that you deserve all the good that life has to offer. Think thoughts that make you happy. Do things that make you feel good. Be with people who make you feel good. Eat things that make your body feel good. Go at a pace that makes you feel good.

## Affirmations for Self-esteem

One of the barriers to allowing positive affirmations to work is feeling "not good enough"—that is, you feel that you don't deserve to have good in your life. Below is a list of self-esteem affirmations. I'd like you to see how many of them you can memorize, and then repeat them often. Doing so will help change that "worthless" feeling you might be carrying around, to one of self-worth. Then watch your positive affirmations materialize.

- I choose to feel good about myself.

- I stand on my own two feet. I accept and use my own power.

- I am totally adequate for all situations.

- It does not matter what other people say or do. What matters is how I choose to react and what I choose to believe about myself.

- I see the world through eyes of love and acceptance. All is well in my world.

- My self-esteem is high because I honor who I am.

- I deserve all that is good.

- My life gets more fabulous every day. I look forward to what each new hour brings.

- I am neither too little nor too much, and I do not have to prove myself to anyone.

- For every problem that I may create, I am confident that I can find a solution.

- Life supports me in every possible way.

- I move through life and know that I am safe—divinely protected and guided.

- I accept others as they are; and they, in turn, accept me.

- I am wonderful, and I feel great. I am grateful for my life.

- I have the self-esteem, power, and confidence to move forward in life with ease.

~

# DAY 4

# Change

Today we're going to explore a topic that many of us find difficult to cope with—change. Although we all want to have our lives change, to have situations become better and easier, we don't want to have to change. We would prefer that *they* change. In order to have this happen, *we must change inside*. We must change our way of thinking, change our way of speaking, change our way of expressing ourselves. Only then will the outer changes occur.

I've always had a streak of stubbornness within me. Even now sometimes when I decide to make a change in my life, this stubbornness can come to the surface, and my resistance to changing *my* thinking is strong. I can temporarily become self-righteous, angry, and withdrawn. Yes, this still goes on within me after all these years of work. It's one of my lessons. However, when this happens now, I know I'm hitting an important point of change. Every time I decide to make a change in my life, to release something else, I'm going ever deeper into myself to do this.

Each old layer must give way in order to be replaced with new thinking. Some of it is easy, and some of it is like trying to lift a boulder with a feather.

The more tenaciously I hold on to an old belief when I say I want to make a change, the more I know this is an important one for me to release. It is only by learning these things that I can teach others.

It is my opinion that many really good teachers do not come from joyful households where all was easy. They come from a place of much pain and suffering, and they've worked through the layers to reach the place where they can now help others to become free. Most good teachers are continually working to release even more, to remove ever-deeper layers of limitation. This becomes a lifetime occupation.

The main difference between the way I used to work at releasing beliefs, and the way I do it today, is that now I don't have to be angry at myself in order to do so. I no longer choose to believe that I'm a bad person just because I find something else to change within me.

The mental work I do now is like cleaning a house. I go through my mental rooms and examine the thoughts and beliefs in them. Some I love, so I polish and shine them and make them even more useful. Some I notice need replacement or repair, and I get around to them as I can. Some are like yesterday's newspapers and old magazines or clothing that's no longer suitable. These I either give away or toss into the trash, and I let them be gone forever. It's not necessary for me to be angry or to feel I'm a bad person in order to do this.

Cleaning the mental house after a lifetime of indulging in negative mental thoughts is a bit like going on a good nutritional program after a lifetime of indulging in junk foods. They both can often create healing crises. As you begin to change your physical diet, the body begins to throw off the accumulation of toxic residue, and as this happens, you can feel rather rotten for a day or two. So it is when you make a decision to change the mental thought patterns—your circumstances can begin to seem worse for a while.

Recall for a moment the end of a Thanksgiving dinner. The food is eaten, and it's time to clean the turkey pan. The pan is all burnt and crusty, so you put in hot water and soap and let it soak for a while. Then you begin to scrape the pan. Now you really have a mess; it looks worse than ever. But, if you just keep scrubbing away, soon you will have a pan as good as new.

It's the same thing with cleaning up a dried-on crusty mental pattern. When we soak it with new ideas, all the gunk comes to the surface to look at.

Now try a very effective method I use with myself and with others.

## Exercise: Willingness to Change

First, go look in a mirror and affirm to yourself, "I am willing to change." Notice how you feel. If you're hesitant or resistant or no longer want to change, ask yourself why. What old belief are you holding on to? Please don't scold yourself, just notice what it is. I'll bet that belief has been causing you a lot of trouble. I wonder where it came from. Do you know?

Whether you know where it came from or not, let's do something to dissolve it, now. Again, go to the mirror, and look deep into your own eyes, touch your throat, and say out loud 10 times, "I am willing to release all resistance."

## AFFIRMATIONS FOR CHANGE

Be willing to allow the changes to happen when they come up in your life. Be aware that where you do not want to change is exactly the area where you need to change the most.

The Universal Intelligence is always responding to your thoughts and words. Things will definitely begin to change as you make these statements.

◆ Changes can begin in this moment. I am willing to see how and where I need to change.

◆ Life brings me only good experiences. I am open to new and wonderful changes.

◆ I release any limitations based on old negative thoughts. I joyfully look forward to the future.

◆ I am safe in the world. I am comfortable with change and growth.

◆ I give myself the green light to go ahead and to joyously embrace the new.

◆ Freedom and change are in the air. I discard old ideas.

◆ I feel reborn. I am free from the past, and I joyously welcome the new.

◆ I open my consciousness to the expansion of life. There is plenty of space for me to grow and change.

◆ Every change in my life can lift me to a new level of understanding.

◆ It is always easy for me to adapt and change. I am flexible and flowing.

◆ I feel safe in the rhythm and flow of ever-changing life.

◆ Every moment presents a wonderful new opportunity to become more of who I am.

◆ I allow change to occur without resistance or fear. I am free.

◆ I am aware that what I do not want to change is exactly what I need to change the most.

◆ Everyone changes and I allow change in everyone.

⌣

# DAY 5

# Fearful Emotions

Today we're going to address fearful emotions. In any given situation, I believe that we have a choice between love and fear. We experience fear of change, fear of not changing, fear of the future, and fear of taking a chance. We fear intimacy, and we fear being alone. We fear letting people know what we need and who we are, and we fear letting go of the past.

At the other end of the spectrum, we have love. Love is the miracle we're all looking for. Loving ourselves works miracles in our lives. I'm not talking about vanity or arrogance, because that's not love.

That's fear. I'm talking about having great respect for ourselves, and gratitude for the miracle of our body and mind.

Remind yourself when you're frightened that you're not loving and trusting yourself. Not feeling "good enough" interferes with the decision-making process. How can you make a good decision when you're not sure about yourself?

Susan Jeffers, in her marvelous book *Feel the Fear and Do It Anyway*, states that "if everybody feels fear when approaching something totally new in life, yet so many are out there 'doing it' despite the fear, then we must conclude that fear is not the problem." She goes on to say that the real issue is not the fear, but how we hold the fear. We can approach it from a position of power or a position of helplessness. The fact that we have the fear becomes irrelevant.

We see what we think the problem is, and then we find out what the real problem is. Not feeling "good enough" and lacking self-love are the real problems.

Emotional problems are among the most painful of all. Occasionally we may feel angry, sad, lonely, guilty, anxious, or frightened. When these feelings take over and become predominant, our lives can become emotional battlegrounds.

What we do with our feelings is important. Are we going to act out in some way? Will we punish others or force our will upon them? Will we somehow abuse ourselves?

The belief that we're not good enough is often at the root of these problems. Good mental health begins with loving the self. When we love and approve of ourselves completely—the good and the so-called bad—we can begin to change.

Part of self-acceptance is releasing other people's opinions. Many of the things we've chosen to believe about ourselves have absolutely no basis in truth and these thoughts have no power over us unless we act upon them. Thoughts are only words strung together. They have no meaning whatsoever. Only we give meaning to them, and we do so by focusing on the negative messages over and over again in our minds. We believe the worst about ourselves. And we choose what kind of meaning we give to our thoughts.

## Exercise: Letting Go

As you read this exercise, take a deep breath, and as you exhale, allow the tension to leave your body. Let your scalp, forehead, and face relax. Your head need not be tense in order to read. Let your tongue, throat, and shoulders relax. Let your back, abdomen, and pelvis relax. Let your breathing be at peace as you relax your legs and feet.

Can you feel a noticeable change in your body since you started reading the previous paragraph? In this relaxed, comfortable position, say to yourself, "I am willing to let go. I release. I let go. I release all tension. I release all fear. I release all anger. I release all guilt. I release all sadness. I let go of old limitations. I let go, and I am at peace. I am at peace with myself. I am at peace with the process of life. I am safe."

Go over this exercise two or three times. Repeat it whenever thoughts of difficulty come up. It takes a little practice for the routine to become a part of you. Once you're familiar with this exercise, you can do it anywhere at any time. You'll be able to relax completely in any situation.

## Exercise: Have Fun with Your Inner Child

When you're in a state of anxiety or fear that keeps you from functioning, you may have abandoned your inner child. Think of some ways in which you can reconnect with your inner child. What could you do for fun? What could you do that is just for you?

List 15 ways in which you could have fun with your inner child. You may enjoy reading good books, going to the movies, gardening, keeping a journal, or taking a hot bath. How about some "childlike" activities? Really take the time to think. You could run on the beach, go to a playground and swing on a swing, draw pictures with crayons, or climb a tree. Once you've made your list, try at least one activity each day. Let the healing begin!

Look at all you've discovered! Keep going—you can create such fun for you and your inner child! Feel the relationship between the two of you healing.

## AFFIRMATIONS FOR
## FEARFUL EMOTIONS

Below I've divided the affirmations for fearful emotions into categories. For each topic there is a sample negative statement, along with an affirmation to counter each belief. However, you may prefer to personalize them by writing down your own greatest fear for each category listed below, and then thinking up a positive affirmation that corresponds to it.

Make these affirmations part of your daily routine. Say them often in the car, at work, while looking in the mirror, or anytime you feel your negative beliefs surfacing.

1.  CAREER
    *Sample Fear*: I'm afraid that no one will ever see my value.

    *Sample Affirmation*: Everybody at work appreciates me.

2.  LIVING SITUATION
    *Sample Fear*: I'll never have a place of my own.

*Sample Affirmation:* There is a perfect home for me, and I accept it now.

3. FAMILY RELATIONS

 *Sample Fear:* My parents won't accept me the way I am.

 *Sample Affirmation:* I accept my parents, and they, in turn, accept and love me.

4. MONEY

 *Sample Fear:* I'm afraid of being poor.

 *Sample Affirmation:* I trust that all my needs will be taken care of.

5. PHYSICAL APPEARANCE

 *Sample Fear:* I think I'm fat and unattractive.

 *Sample Affirmation:* I release the need to criticize my body.

6. SEX

 *Sample Fear:* I'm afraid that I'll have to "perform."

 *Sample Affirmation:* I am relaxed, and I flow with life easily and effortlessly.

7. HEALTH

 *Sample Fear:* I'm afraid I'll get sick and won't be able to take care of myself.

*Sample Affirmation*: I always attract all the help I need.

8. RELATIONSHIPS

*Sample Fear*: I don't think anyone will ever love me.

*Sample Affirmation*: Love and acceptance are mine. I love myself.

9. OLD AGE

*Sample Fear*: I'm afraid of getting old.

*Sample Affirmation*: Every age has its infinite possibilities.

10. DEATH AND DYING

*Sample Fear*: What if there's no life after death?

*Sample Affirmation*: I trust the process of life. I am on an endless journey through eternity.

11. GENERAL

*Sample Fear*: I'm anxious all the time.

*Sample Affirmation*: I am at peace.

*Sample Fear*: People scare me.

*Sample Affirmation*: I am loved and safe wherever I go.

*Sample Fear:* I have difficulty expressing my feelings.

*Sample Affirmation:* It is safe for me to express my feelings.

*Sample Fear:* I feel like a failure.

*Sample Affirmation:* My life is a success.

*Sample Fear:* I'm scared of being alone.

*Sample Affirmation:* I express love, and always attract love wherever I go.

# DAY 6

# Critical Thinking

Today we're going to look at our inner critic—the little voice inside that perpetually criticizes what we think and do. Is your inner voice constantly picking, picking, picking? Are you seeing the world through critical eyes? Do you judge everything? Do you stand in self-righteousness?

Most of us have such a strong tendency to judge and criticize that we can't easily break the habit. However, it's the most important issue to work on immediately. We'll never be able to really love ourselves until we go beyond the need to make life wrong.

As a little baby, you were so open to life. You looked at the world with eyes of wonder. Unless something was scary or someone harmed you, you accepted life just as it was. Later, as you grew up, you began to accept the opinions of others and make them your own. You learned how to criticize.

## Exercise:
## Let Go of Critical Thinking

Let's examine some of your beliefs about critical thinking. Answer the following questions and write down your answers. Be as open and honest as you can.

- What was your family pattern?

- What did you learn about criticism from your mother?

- What were the things she criticized?

- Did she criticize you? If so, for what?

- When was your father judgmental?

- Did he judge himself?

- How did your father judge you?

- Was it a family pattern to criticize each other? If so, how and when did your family members do so?

- When is the first time you remember being criticized?

- How did your family judge your neighbors?

Now answer the following questions and write down your answers:

- Did you have loving, supportive teachers at school, or were they always telling you what was lacking in you? What sort of things did they tell you?

- Can you begin to see where you might have picked up a pattern of being critical? Who was the most critical person in your childhood?

Now read back through your answers and think about them. I believe that criticism shrivels our spirits. It only reinforces the belief that we're "not good enough." It certainly doesn't bring out the best in us.

---

## Exercise: Support Your Inner Child

In order for a child to grow and blossom, he or she needs love, acceptance, and praise. We can be shown "better" ways to do things without making the way we do it "wrong." The child within you still needs that love and approval.

You can say the following positive statements to your inner child:

- I love you and know that you're doing the best you can.

- You're perfect just as you are.

- You become more wonderful every day.

- I approve of you.

- Let's see if we can find a better way to do this.

- Growing and changing is fun, and we can do it together.

These are words that children want to hear. It makes them feel good. When they feel good, they do their best. They unfold beautifully.

If your child, or your inner child, is used to constantly being "wrong," it may take a while for him or her to accept the new, positive words. If you make a definite decision to release criticism and you're consistent, you can work miracles.

Give yourself one month to talk to your inner child in positive ways. Use the affirmations listed above, or make up a list of your own. Carry a list of these affirmations with you. When you notice yourself becoming judgmental, take out the list and read it two or three times. Better yet, speak it aloud in front of a mirror.

## Exercise: Your Critical Self

Whereas criticism breaks down the inner spirit and never changes a thing, praise builds up the spirit and can bring about positive change. Write down two ways in which you criticize yourself in the area of love and intimacy. Perhaps you're not able to tell people how you feel or what you need. Maybe you have a fear of relationships, or you attract partners who hurt you. Then, think of something you can praise yourself for in this area.

For example:

> *I criticize myself for:* Choosing people who aren't able to give me what I need, and for being clingy in relationships.

> *I praise myself for:* Being able to tell someone that I like him/her (it scared me, yet I did it anyway); and for allowing myself to be openly loving and affectionate.

Now think of things you criticize yourself for and ways you can praise yourself in other areas.

Congratulations! You've just begun to break another old habit! You're learning to praise yourself—in this moment. And the point of power is always in the present moment.

## Exercise: Mirror Work

As I have mentioned before, mirror work is simple and very powerful. It simply involves looking into a mirror when you say your affirmations. Mirrors reflect your true feelings back to you. As children, you received most of your negative messages from adults, many of them looking you straight in the eye and perhaps even shaking a finger at you.

Today, when most of us look into a mirror, we'll say something negative. We either criticize our looks, or berate ourselves for something else.

To look yourself in the eye and make a positive declaration is one of the quickest ways to get positive results with affirmations. So, right now, think of a person whom you're angry with. Sit down in front of a mirror. Be sure to have some tissues nearby. Look into your own eyes and "see" the other person. Tell this person what you're so angry about.

When you're finished, tell him or her, "What I really want is your love and approval." We're all seeking love and approval. That's what we want from everyone, and that's what everyone wants from us. Love and approval bring harmony into our lives.

In order to be free, you need to release the old ties that bind you. So once again, look into the mirror and affirm to yourself, "I am willing to release the need to be an angry person." Notice if you're really willing to let go, or if you're holding on to the past.

## AFFIRMATIONS FOR CRITICAL THINKING

Make the following affirmations part of your daily routine. Say them often in the car, at work, while looking in the mirror, or anytime you feel your negative beliefs surfacing.

- Everybody is doing the best they can, including me.

- I release the need to criticize others.

- I only speak positively about those in my world. Negativity has no part in my life.

- I become more proficient every day.

- I allow myself freedom with all my emotions.

- Healthy expressions of anger keep me healthy.

- I express my anger in appropriate places and ways.

- I give myself permission to acknowledge my feelings.

- All of my emotions are acceptable.

- ◆ I comfort my inner child, and we are safe.

- ◆ I am safe with all of my emotions.

- ◆ The more honest I am, the more I am loved.

- ◆ My opinions are valued.

- ◆ I respect others for being different, but not wrong. We are all one.

- ◆ I am willing to release all patterns of criticism.

~

# DAY 7

# Letting Go of the Past

Today we're going to look at affirmations to help us let go of the past and move on. The past is over and done and cannot be changed. This—the here and now—is the only moment we can experience. Even when we lament about the past, we're experiencing our memory of it in this moment, and losing the real experience of this moment in the process.

Many people come to me and say they cannot enjoy today because of something that happened in the past. Because they did not do something or do it in a certain way in the past, they cannot live a full life today. Because they no longer have something they had in the past, they cannot enjoy today. Because they were hurt in the past, they will not accept love now, and so on. These negative statements simply keep them powerless to live their lives in the here and now.

Here are some more specific examples. Do any of them resonate with you?

- Because I did not get invited to the high school prom, I cannot enjoy life today.

- Because I did poorly at my first audition, I will be terrified of auditions forever.

- Because I am no longer married, I cannot live a full life today.

- Because I was hurt by a remark once, I will never trust anyone again.

- Because I stole something once, I must punish myself forever.

- Because I was poor as a child, I will never get anywhere.

What we often refuse to realize is that holding on to the past—no matter what it was or how awful it was—is *only hurting us.* "They" really don't care. Usually, "they" are not even aware. We are only hurting ourselves by refusing to live in this moment to the fullest.

Let us now clean up the past in our minds. We need to release the emotional attachment to it. Allow the memories to be just memories.

If you think back to what you used to wear in the third grade, usually there is no emotional attachment. It's just a memory.

It can be the same for all of the past events in our lives. As we let go, we become free to use all of our mental power to enjoy this moment and to create a great future.

You don't have to keep punishing yourself for the past. List all of the things you're willing to let go of.

- How willing are you to let go? Notice your reactions, and write them down.

- What will you have to do to let these things go? How willing are you to do so?

- For each thing you wrote down on your list, write a positive affirmation to help you release it.

## Exercise: Letting Go

We have already practiced this exercise in Day 5—it's also helpful to use in this context of letting go of the past.

As you read this, take a deep breath and, as you exhale, allow all the tension to leave your body. Let your scalp and your forehead and your face relax. Your head does not need to be tense in order for you to read. Let your tongue and your throat and your shoulders relax. You can hold a book with relaxed arms and hands. Do that now. Let your back and your abdomen and your pelvis relax. Let your breathing be at peace as you relax your legs and feet.

Is there a big change in your body since you began the previous paragraph? Notice how much you hold on. If you are doing it with your body, you are doing it with your mind.

In this relaxed, comfortable position, say to yourself, "I am willing to let go. I release. I let go. I release all tension. I release all fear. I release all anger. I release all guilt. I release all sadness. I let go of all old limitations. I let go, and I am at peace. I am at peace with myself. I am at peace with the process of life. I am safe."

Go over this exercise two or three times. Feel the ease of letting go. Repeat it whenever you feel thoughts of difficulty coming up. It takes a little practice for the routine to become a part of you. When you put yourself into this peaceful state first, it becomes easy for your affirmations to take hold. You become open and receptive to them. There is no need to struggle or stress or strain. Just relax and think the appropriate thoughts. Yes, it is this easy.

## Exercise: Physical Releasing

Sometimes we need to experience a physical letting go. Experiences and emotions can get locked in the body. Screaming in the car with all the windows rolled up can be very releasing if we have been stifling our verbal expression. Beating the bed or kicking pillows is another harmless way to release pent-up anger or frustration. If you feel embarrassed or inhibited by the idea of expressing yourself so physically, say to yourself: "I give myself permission to acknowledge my feelings and release past experiences." Or if this is really not your style, play a sport such as tennis, or go running.

A while ago, I had a pain in my shoulder for a day or two. I tried to ignore it, but it wouldn't go away. Finally, I sat down and asked myself, "What is happening here? What am I feeling?"

I realized, "It feels like burning. Burning… burning… that means anger. What are you angry about?"

I couldn't think of what I was angry about, so I said, "Well, let's see if we can find out." I put two large pillows on the bed and began to hit them with a lot of energy.

After about 12 hits, I realized exactly what I was angry about. It was so clear. So I beat the pillows even harder and made some noise and released the emotions from my body. When I got through, I felt much better, and the next day my shoulder was fine.

## AFFIRMATIONS FOR LETTING GO OF THE PAST

Make these affirmations part of your daily routine. Say them often in the car, at work, while looking in the mirror, or anytime you feel your negative beliefs surfacing.

- The past is over and cannot be changed. This is the only moment I can experience.

- I now choose to release every negative, destructive, fearful idea and thought from my mind and my life.

- It is healing to show my emotions. It is safe for me to be vulnerable.

- I release the need to blame anyone, including myself.

- My heart is open. I am willing to release all resistance.

- I now release anger in positive ways. I love and appreciate myself.

- I move beyond old limitations and now express myself freely and creatively.

- I am willing to release the need to be unworthy. I am becoming all that I am destined to be.

- It is safe for me to go beyond my parents' limitations. I am free to be me.

- I release all struggle now, and I am at peace.

- I release any limitations based on old, negative thoughts. I joyfully look forward to the future.

- I say "Out!' to every negative thought about the past that comes into my mind.

- I release any feelings of competition or comparison from the past.

~

# DAY 8

# Forgiveness

Forgiveness, our topic for today, is a difficult area for so many people. We all need to do forgiveness work. Anyone who has a problem with loving themselves is stuck in this area. Forgiveness opens our hearts to self-love. Many of us carry grudges for years and years. We feel self-righteous because of what they did to us. I call this being stuck in the prison of self-righteous resentment. We get to be right. We never get to be happy.

I can almost hear you saying, "But you don't know what they did to me; it's unforgivable." Being unwilling to forgive is a terrible thing to do to yourself. Bitterness is like swallowing a teaspoon of poison every day. It accumulates and harms you. It's impossible to be healthy and free when you keep yourself bound to the past. The incident is long gone and over with. Yes, it's true that they didn't behave well. However, it's over. You might feel that if you forgive them, then you're saying that what they did to you was okay.

One of our biggest spiritual lessons is to understand that everyone is doing the best they can at any given moment. People can only do so much with the understanding, awareness, and knowledge that they have. Invariably, anyone who mistreats someone was mistreated themselves as a child. The greater the violence, the greater their own inner pain, and the more they may lash out. This is not to say that their behavior is acceptable or excusable. However, for our own spiritual growth, we must be aware of their pain.

The incident is over. Perhaps long over. Let it go. Allow yourself to be free. Come out of prison, and step into the sunshine of life. If the incident is still going on, then ask yourself why you think so little of yourself that you still put up with it. Why do you stay in such a situation? Don't waste time trying to "get even." It doesn't work. What you give out always comes back to you. So drop the past and work on loving yourself in the now. Then you'll have a wonderful future.

That person who is the hardest to forgive is the one who can teach you the greatest lessons. When you love yourself enough to rise above the old situation, then understanding and forgiveness will be easy. And you'll be free. Does freedom frighten you? Does it feel safer to be stuck in your old resentment and bitterness?

## Exercise:
## Family Attitudes

- Was your mother a forgiving person?

- Was your father?

- Was bitterness a way of handling hurtful situations in your family?

- How did your mother get even?

- What about your father?

- How do you get even?

- Do you feel good when you get revenge?

- Why do you feel this way?

An interesting phenomenon is that when you do your own forgiveness work, other people often respond to it. It's not necessary to go to the persons involved and tell them you forgive them. Sometimes you'll want to do this, but you don't have to. The major work in forgiveness is done in your own heart.

Forgiveness is seldom for "them." It's for us. The person you need to forgive may even be dead.

I've heard from many people who have truly forgiven someone, and then a month or two later, they may receive a phone call or a letter from the other person, asking to be forgiven. This seems to be particularly true when forgiveness exercises are done in front of a mirror, so as you do this exercise, notice how deep your feelings might be.

## Exercise: Mirror Work for Forgiveness

Mirror work is often uncomfortable and something you may want to avoid. I believe that you receive the most benefits if you sit in front of a mirror. I like to use the big dressing mirror on the back of my bedroom door. I settle in with a box of tissues.

Give yourself time to do this exercise, or you can do it over and over. Most likely you have lots of people to forgive.

Sit in front of your mirror. Close your eyes, and breathe deeply several times. Think of the many people who have hurt you in your life. Let them pass through your mind. Now open your eyes and begin talking to one of them.

Say something like: "You've hurt me deeply. However, I won't stay stuck in the past any longer. I am willing to forgive you." Take a breath and then say, "I forgive you, and I set you free." Breathe again and say, "You are free, and I am free."

Notice how you feel. You may feel resistance, or you may feel clear. If you feel resistance, just breathe and say, "I am willing to release all resistance."

This may be a day when you can forgive several people. It may be a day when you can forgive only one. It doesn't matter. No matter how you're doing this exercise, it's perfect for you. Forgiveness can be like peeling away the layers of an onion. If there are too many layers, put the onion away for a day. You can always come back and peel another layer. Acknowledge yourself for being willing to even begin this exercise.

As you continue to do this exercise, today or another day, expand your list of those to forgive. Remember:

- family members

- teachers

- kids at school

- lovers

- friends

- co-workers

- government agencies or figures

- church members or personnel

- medical professionals

- God

- other authority figures

- yourself

Most of all, forgive yourself. Stop being so hard on yourself. Self-punishment isn't necessary. You were doing the very best you could.

As you continue to do this exercise, you'll find burdens melting off your shoulders. You may be surprised by the amount of old baggage you've been carrying. Be gentle with yourself as you go through the cleansing process.

## AFFIRMATIONS FOR FORGIVENESS

Make these affirmations part of your daily routine. Say them often in the car, at work, while looking in the mirror, or anytime you feel your negative beliefs surfacing.

- This is a new moment. I am free to let go.

- I take responsibility for my own life. I am free.

- I learn to forgive and release. Inner peace is my goal.

- People do the best they can with the knowledge, understanding, and awareness that they have at the time.

- I am grown up now, and I take loving care of my inner child.

- I forgive others, and I now create my life in the way I wish it to be.

- My spiritual growth is not dependent on others.

- Forgiving makes me feel free and light.

- I release myself from prison. I am safe and free.

- It is empowering to forgive and let go.

- There is no right or wrong. I move beyond my judgment.

- I am willing to go beyond my own limitations.

- My parents treated me in the way they had been treated. I forgive them—and their parents, too.

- I refuse to limit myself. I am always willing to take the next step.

- I give myself permission to let go.

# DAY 9

# Health

Health is an extremely important topic, which is why we are going to be exploring it over the next two days.

I believe that we live in a "yes" Universe. No matter what we choose to believe or think, the Universe always says yes to us. So we want to think and believe that we have the right to be healthy, that health is natural to us. The Universe will support and say yes to this belief. Be a "yes" person, and know that you live in a "yes" world, being responded to by a "yes" Universe.

Be very clear that your body is always trying to maintain a state of optimal health, no matter how badly you treat it. If you take good care of your body, it will reward you with vibrant health and energy.

I believe that we contribute to every "illness" in our body. The body, as with everything else in life, is a mirror of our inner thoughts and beliefs. Our body is always talking to us, if we will only take the time to listen. Every cell within our bodies responds to every single thought we think.

When we discover what the mental pattern is behind an illness, we have a chance to change the pattern and, therefore, the dis-ease. Most people don't want to be sick on a conscious level, yet every dis-ease that we have is a teacher. Illness is the body's way of telling us that there's a false idea in our consciousness. Something that we're believing, saying, doing, or thinking is not for our highest good. I always picture the body tugging at us saying, "Please—pay attention!"

Sometimes people do want to be sick. In our society, we've made illness a legitimate way to avoid responsibility or unpleasant situations. If we can't learn to say no, then we may have to invent a dis-ease to say no for us.

I read an interesting report a few years back. It stated that only 30 percent of patients follow their doctor's instructions. According to Dr. John Harrison, author of the fascinating book *Love Your Disease*, many people go to doctors only to have their acute symptoms relieved—so that they can tolerate their dis-ease. It's as if an unwritten, subconscious agreement exists between doctor and patient: The doctor agrees not to cure the patient if the patient pretends to do something about his or her condition.

Also in this agreement, one person generally gets to pay, and the other becomes the authority figure... and so, both parties are satisfied.

True healing involves body, mind, and spirit. I believe that if we "cure" an illness yet do not address the emotional and spiritual issues that surround that ailment, it will only manifest again.

## Exercise: Releasing Your Health Problems

Are you willing to release the need that has contributed to your health problems? Once again, when you have a condition that you want to change, the first thing that you have to do is say so. Say: "I am willing to release the need in me that has created this condition." Say it again. Say it looking in the mirror. Say it every time you think about your condition. It's the first step in creating a change. Now, do the following:

- List all of your mother's illnesses.

- List all of your father's illnesses.

- List all of your illnesses.

- Do you see a connection?

## Exercise: Health and Dis-ease

Let's examine some of your beliefs about health and dis-ease. Answer the following questions. Be as open and honest as you can.

- What do you remember about your childhood illnesses?

- What did you learn from your parents about illness?

- What, if anything, did you enjoy about being sick as a child?

- Is there a belief about illness from your childhood that you're still acting on today?

- How have you contributed to the state of your health?

- Would you like your health to change? If so, in what way?

## Exercise: Your Beliefs about Sickness

Complete the following statements as honestly as you can.

- The way I make myself sick is…

- I get sick when I try to avoid…

- When I get sick, I always want to…

- When I was sick as a child, my mother always…

- My greatest fear when I'm sick is that…

## Exercise: Intensifying the Power of Affirmations

Writing an affirmation can intensify its power, so I'd like you to write out a positive affirmation about your health 25 times. You may create your own, or use one of the following:

- My healing is already in process.

- I deserve good health.

- I listen with love to my body's messages.

- My health is radiant, vibrant, and dynamic now.

- I am grateful for my perfect health.

## Exercise: Deserving Good Health

Let's examine the issue of self-worth with respect to your health. Answer the following questions, then create a positive affirmation to counter each one if your response was a negative one.

**1. Do I deserve good health?**

*Sample Answer*: No. Illness runs in my family.

*Sample Affirmation*: I accept and deserve perfect health now.

2. **What do I fear most about my health?**

*Sample Answer*: I'm afraid that I'll get sick and die.
*Sample Affirmation*: It is safe to be well now. I am always loved.

3. **What am I "getting" from this belief?**

*Sample Answer*: I don't have to be responsible or go to work.
*Sample Affirmation*: I am confident and secure. Life is easy for me.

4. **What do I fear will happen if I let go of this belief?**

*Sample Answer*: I'll have to grow up.
*Sample Affirmation*: It is safe for me to be an adult.

## Affirmations for Health

Make these affirmations part of your daily routine. Say them often in the car, at work, while looking in the mirror, or anytime you feel your negative beliefs surfacing.

- My body heals rapidly.

- My body is ideal for me in this lifetime.

- I love every cell of my body.

- I am filled with energy and enthusiasm.

- I am healthy and whole and filled with joy.

- Good health is mine now. I release the past.

- I go within and connect with that part of myself that knows how to heal.

- I am the only person who has control over my eating habits. I can always resist something if I choose to.

- Filling my mind with pleasant thoughts is the quickest road to health.

- ◆ I allow life and vitality to flow through me.

- ◆ I am grateful for my healthy body. I love life.

- ◆ My body uses relaxation as a time to repair and rejuvenate itself. The more I relax, the healthier I am.

- ◆ I take brisk walks in the sunshine to invigorate my body and soul.

- ◆ I am gentle with my body. I love myself.

- ◆ I give myself permission to be well.

~

# DAY 10

# More on Health

Yesterday we looked at how our beliefs about sickness affect our health. Today we learn how we can influence our health positively through the power of our thoughts.

If you want to create better health in your body, there are definitely some things you must not do: You must not get angry at your body for any reason. Anger is another affirmation, and it's telling your body that you hate it, or parts of it. Your cells are very aware of every thought you have. Think of your body as a servant that's working as hard as it can to keep you in perfect health no matter how you treat it.

Your body knows how to heal itself. If you feed it healthy foods and beverages, give it exercise and sufficient sleep, and think happy thoughts, then its work is easy. The cells are working in a happy, healthy atmosphere. However, if you're a couch potato who feeds your body junk food and lots of diet soda, and you skimp on sleep and are grouchy and irritable all the time, then the cells in your body are working at a disadvantage—they're in a disagreeable atmosphere. If this is the case, it's no wonder that your body isn't as healthy as you'd like it to be.

You'll never create good health by talking or thinking about your illness. Good health comes from love and appreciation. You want to put as much love into your body as you possibly can. Talk to it and stroke it in loving ways. If there's a part of your body that's ailing or dis-eased, then you want to treat it as you would a sick little child. Tell it how much you love it, and that you're doing everything you can to help it get well quickly.

If you're sick, then you want to do more than just go to the doctor and have him or her give you a chemical to take care of the symptom. Your body is telling you that something you're doing isn't good for your body. You need to learn more about health—the more you learn, the easier it is to take care of your body. You don't want to choose to feel like a victim. If you do, you'll just be giving your power away. You could go to a health-food store and pick up one of the many good books that teach you how to keep yourself healthy, or you could see a nutritionist and have a healthy diet created just for you, but whatever you do, create a healthy, happy mental atmosphere. Be a willing participant in your own health plan.

I believe that we create every so-called illness in our body. The body, like everything else in life, is a mirror of our inner thoughts and beliefs. Our body is always talking to us; we just need to take the time to listen. Every cell within our body responds to every single thought we think and every word we speak.

Continuous modes of thinking and speaking produce body behaviors and postures and "eases," or dis-eases. The person who has a permanently scowling face didn't produce that by having joyous, loving thoughts. Older people's faces and bodies so clearly show a lifetime of thinking patterns. How will you look when you're elderly?

Learn to accept that your life is not a series of random events, but a pathway of awakening. If you live every day in this way, you'll never grow old. You'll just keep growing. Imagine the day you turn 49 as the infancy of another life. A woman who reaches age 50 today and remains free of cancer and heart disease can expect to see her 92nd birthday. You and only you have the ability to customize your own life cycle. So change your thinking now and get going! You're here for a very important reason, and everything you need is available to you.

You can choose to think thoughts that create a mental atmosphere that contributes to illness, or you can choose to think thoughts that create a healthy atmosphere both within you and around you. (My book *Heal Your Body* is a comprehensive guide to the metaphysical causes of dis-ease, and it includes all the affirmations you'll need to overcome any specific ailment.)

## MORE AFFIRMATIONS FOR HEALTH

Make these affirmations part of your daily routine. Say them often in the car, at work, while looking in the mirror, or anytime you feel your negative beliefs surfacing.

- ◆ I enjoy the foods that are best for my body.

- ◆ I look forward to a healthy old age because I take loving care of my body now.

- ◆ I am constantly discovering new ways to improve my health.

- ◆ I return my body to optimal health by giving it what it needs on every level.

- ◆ I am pain free and totally in sync with life.

- ◆ Healing happens! I get my mind out of the way and allow the intelligence of my body to do its healing work naturally.

- ◆ I balance my life between work, rest, and play. They all get equal time.

- I am willing to ask for help when I need it. I always choose the health professional who is just right for my needs.

- I breathe deeply and fully. I take in the breath of life, and I am nourished.

- I get plenty of sleep every night. My body appreciates how I take care of it.

- I lovingly do everything I can to assist my body in maintaining perfect health.

- Perfect health is my Divine right, and I claim it now.

- I devote a portion of my time to helping others. It is good for my own health.

- Water is my favorite beverage. I drink lots of water to cleanse my body and mind.

- My happy thoughts help create my healthy body.

# DAY 11

# Loving Yourself

Time and again I have discovered that no matter what the problem is, the main issue comes back to *loving the self.* This is our topic for today. Working at this is the "magic wand" that dissolves problems. Remember the times when you have felt good about yourself and how well your life was going? Remember the times when you were in love and for those periods you seemed to have no problems? Well, loving yourself is going to bring such a surge of good feelings and good fortune to you that you'll be dancing on air. Loving yourself *makes you feel good.*

It is impossible to really love yourself unless you have self-approval and self-acceptance. This means no criticism whatsoever. I can hear all the objections right now.

"But I have always criticized myself." "How can I possibly like that about myself?" "My parents/ teachers/lovers always criticized me." "How will I be motivated?" "But it is wrong for me to do those things." "How am I going to change if I don't criticize myself?"

Self-criticism such as that illustrated above is just the mind going on with old chatter. See how you have trained your mind to berate you and be resistant to change? Ignore those thoughts and get on with the important work at hand!

Let's go back to an exercise we did earlier (*see Day 3*). Look into the mirror again, and say, "I approve of myself." How does that feel now? Is it a little easier after the work we have done? This is still the main issue. Self-approval and self-acceptance are the keys to positive changes.

Part of self-acceptance is releasing other people's opinions. If I were with you and kept telling you,

"You are a purple pig, you are a purple pig." You would either laugh at me, or get annoyed with me and think I was crazy. It would be most unlikely that you would think it was true. Yet many of the things we have chosen to believe about ourselves are just as far out and untrue. To believe that your self-worth is dependent on the shape of your body is your version of believing that "You are a purple pig."

Often what we think of as the things "wrong" with us are only our expressions of our own individuality. This is our uniqueness and what is special about us. Nature never repeats itself. Since time began on this planet, there have never been two snowflakes alike or two raindrops the same. And every daisy is different from every other daisy. Our fingerprints are different, and we are different. We are meant to be different. When we can accept this, then there is no competition and no comparison. To try to be like another is to shrivel our soul. We have come to this planet to express who we are.

I didn't even know who I was until I began to learn to love myself as I am in this moment.

## Exercise: I Love Myself

Take your pad of paper and at the top write, "I love myself; therefore…"

Finish this sentence in as many ways as you can. Read it over daily, and add to it as you think of new things.

If you can work with a partner, do so. Hold hands and alternate saying, "I love myself; therefore…" The biggest benefit of doing this exercise is that you learn it is almost impossible to belittle yourself when you say you love yourself.

There's a big difference between the need for love, and being needy for love. When you're needy for love, it means that you're missing love and approval from the most important person you know—yourself. The first relationship to improve is the one you have with yourself. When you're happy with yourself, then all of your other relationships improve, too. A happy person is very attractive to others. If you're looking for more love, then you need to love yourself more. This means no criticism, no complaining, no blaming, no whining, and no choosing to feel lonely. It means being very content with yourself in the present moment and choosing to think thoughts that make you feel good now.

If something unpleasant happens to you during the day, immediately go to the mirror and say: "I love you anyway." Events come and go, but the love you have for yourself can be constant, and it's the most important quality you possess in life. If something wonderful happens, go to the mirror and say, "Thank you." Acknowledge yourself for creating this wonderful experience.

First thing in the morning and last thing in the evening, I want you to look into your eyes and say: "I love you, I really love you. And I accept you exactly as you are." It can be tough at first, but if you stick with it, in a short time this affirmation will be true for you.

You'll find that as your self-love grows, so will your self-respect, and any changes that you find yourself needing to make will be easier to accomplish when you know that they're the right ones for you. Love is never outside yourself—it's always within you. As you're more loving, you'll be more lovable.

I suggest that you work on loving yourself nonstop. Demonstrate the growing love you have for yourself. Treat yourself to romance and love. Show yourself how special you are. Pamper yourself. Buy yourself flowers for your home; and surround yourself with colors, textures, and scents that please you. Life always mirrors back to us the feelings we have inside.

If you want to go from loneliness thinking to fulfillment thinking, then you need to think in terms of creating a loving mental atmosphere within you and around you. When you truly love who you are, you stay centered, calm, and secure, and your relationships at home as well as at work are wonderful. You'll find yourself reacting to various situations and people differently. Matters that once may have been desperately important won't seem quite as crucial anymore. New people will enter your life, and perhaps some old ones will disappear—this can be kind of scary at first—but it can also be wonderful, refreshing, and exciting.

## Affirmations for Loving Yourself

Make these affirmations part of your daily routine. Say them often in the car, at work, while looking in the mirror, or anytime you feel your negative beliefs surfacing.

* I am worthy of my own love.

* I am loved and accepted exactly as I am, right here and right now.

* My consciousness is filled with healthy, positive loving thoughts that reflect themselves in my experience.

* The greatest gift I can give myself is unconditional love.

- I no longer wait to be perfect in order to love myself.

- I love myself exactly as I am.

- I look terrific and feel terrific. Here I am world—open and receptive to all good!

- Love is the miracle cure. Loving myself works miracles in my life.

- I see myself as beautiful, lovable, and appreciated. I am proud to be me.

- I know that before others will love me, I have to love myself. My self-love begins now.

- I am gentle, kind, and patient with myself. Those around me reflect this tender care.

- I am the most important person in my life.

- I look within to find my treasures.

- I am now willing to see my own beauty and magnificence.

- I love who I am, and reward myself with thoughts of praise.

~

# DAY 12

# Friendship

Today we're going to look at friendship, which can be the basis for our most enduring and important relationships. We can live without lovers or spouses. We can live without our primary families. But most of us cannot live happily without friends. I believe that we choose our parents before we're born into this planet, but we choose our friends on a more conscious level.

Ralph Waldo Emerson, the great American philosopher and writer, wrote an essay on friendship, calling it the "nectar of God." He explained that in romantic relationships, one person is always trying to change the other, but friends can stand back and look at one another with appreciation and respect.

Friends can be an extension or a substitute for the nuclear family. There's a great need in most of us to share life experiences with others. Not only do we learn more about others when we engage in friendship, but we can also learn more about ourselves. These relationships are mirrors of our self-worth and self-esteem. They afford us the perfect opportunity to look at ourselves, and the areas where we might need to grow.

When the bond between friends becomes strained, we can look to the negative messages of childhood. It may be time for mental housecleaning. Cleaning the mental house after a lifetime of negative messages is a bit like starting a sound nutritional program after a lifetime of eating junk foods. As you change your diet, your body will throw off a toxic residue, and you may feel worse for a day or two.

So it is when you make a decision to change your mental thought patterns. Your circumstances may worsen for a while, but remember—you may have to dig through a lot of dry weed to get to the rich soil below. But you can do it! I know you can!

## Exercise:
## Explore Your Friendships

Write down the following affirmation three times, then answer the questions that follow.

*"I am willing to release any pattern within me that creates troubled friendships."*

- What were your first childhood friendships like?

- How are your friendships today like those childhood friendships?

- What did you learn about friendship from your parents?

- What kinds of friends did your parents have?

- What kinds of friends would you like to have in the future? Be specific.

## Exercise: Self-worth and Friendship

Let's examine your self-worth in the area of friendship. Answer each of the following questions below. Then, write a positive affirmation (in the present tense) to replace the old belief.

1. **Do I feel worthy of having good friends?**

   *Sample Answer*: No. Why would anyone want to be around me?

   *Sample Affirmation*: I love and accept myself, and I am a magnet for friends.

2. **What do I fear most about having close friends?**

   *Sample Answer*: I am afraid of betrayal. I don't feel that I can trust anyone.

   *Sample Affirmation*: I trust myself, I trust life, and I trust my friends.

3. **What am I "getting" from this belief?**

   *Sample Answer*: I get to be judgmental. I wait for my friends to make one false move so that I can show them that they're wrong.

   *Sample Affirmation*: All of my friendships are successful. I am a loving and nurturing friend.

4.  **What do I fear will happen if I let go of this belief?**

    *Sample Answer*: I'll lose control. I'd have to let people really get to know me.

    *Sample Affirmation*: Loving others is easy when I love and accept myself.

If we're all responsible for the events in our lives, then there's no one to blame. Whatever is happening "out there" is only a reflection of our own inner thinking.

## Exercise: Thinking about Your Friends

Think of three events in your life where you feel you were mistreated or abused by friends. Perhaps a friend betrayed a confidence or abandoned you in a time of need. Maybe this person interfered with a spouse or mate.

In each case, name the event, and write down the thoughts you had at the time that preceded each event.

*Sample Event*: When I was 16 years old, my best friend Susie turned on me and started to spread vicious rumors. When I tried to confront her, she lied to me. I was friendless my entire senior year.

*Sample Thoughts*: I did not deserve friends. I was drawn to my friend Susie because she was cold and judgmental. I was used to being judged and criticized.

## Exercise: The Support of Your Friends

Now, think of three times in your life when you were supported by friends. Perhaps a good friend stood up for you or gave you money when you needed it. Maybe this person helped you resolve a difficult situation.

In each case, name the event, and write down the thoughts you had at the time that preceded each event.

*Sample Event*: I'll always remember Helen. When people at my first job were making fun of me because I said something stupid at a meeting, Helen stood up for me. She helped me through my embarrassment and saved my job.

*My Deepest Thoughts Were*: Even if I make a mistake, someone will always help me. I deserve to be supported.

## Visualizations

Which friends do you need to acknowledge? Take a moment to visualize them. Look those people in the eye and say: "I thank you and bless you with love for being there for me when I needed you. May your life be filled with joy."

Which friends do you need to forgive? Take a moment to visualize them. Look at those people in the eye and say: "I forgive you for not acting the way I wanted you to. I forgive you and I set you free."

### AFFIRMATIONS FOR FRIENDSHIP

Make these affirmations part of your daily routine. Say them often in the car, at work, while looking in the mirror, or anytime you feel your negative beliefs surfacing.

- ◆ I give myself permission to be a friend.

- ◆ My friends are loving and supportive.

◆ As I release all criticism, judgmental people leave my life.

◆ I am open and receptive to all points of view.

◆ I respect others, and they respect me.

◆ My love and acceptance of others creates lasting friendships.

◆ It is safe for me to be open.

◆ I leave my friends alone. We both have total freedom to be ourselves.

◆ I trust my inner wisdom to guide me.

◆ It is safe for me to ask for what I want.

◆ I move beyond those limitations and express myself honestly.

◆ Knowing that friends were once strangers to me, I welcome new people into my life.

◆ Loving people fill my life, and I find myself easily expressing love to others.

◆ The people in my life are really mirrors of me. My world is safe and friendly.

◆ A smiling face and joyful, loving words are the best presents I can share with everyone I know.

# DAY 13

# Love and Intimacy

Today we will explore love and our more intimate relationships. We have relationships with everything. You are even having a relationship now with this book, and with me and my concepts.

The relationships you have with objects and foods and weather and transportation and with people all reflect the relationship you have with yourself. The relationship you have with yourself is highly influenced by the relationships you had with the adults around you as a child. The way the adults reacted to us then is often the way we react toward ourselves now, both positively and negatively.

Sondra Ray, the great rebirther who has done so much work with relationships, claims that every major relationship we have is a reflection of the relationship we had with one of our parents. She also claims that until we clean up that first one, we will never be free to create exactly what we want in relationships.

Relationships are mirrors of ourselves. What we attract always mirrors either qualities we have or beliefs we have about relationships. This is true whether it is a boss, a co-worker, an employee, a friend, a lover, a spouse, or a child. The things you don't like about these people are either what you yourself do or would not do, or what you believe. You could not attract them or have them in your life if the way they are didn't somehow complement your own life.

We attract love when we least expect it, when we're not looking for it. Hunting for love never brings the right partner. It only creates longing and unhappiness. Love is never outside ourselves; love is within us.

Don't insist that love come immediately. Perhaps you are not ready for it, or you are not developed enough to attract the love you want. Don't settle for anybody just to have someone. Set your standards. What kind of love do you want to attract? List the qualities in yourself, and you'll attract a person who has them. You might examine what may be keeping love away. Could it be criticism? Feelings of unworthiness? Unreasonable standards? Movie star images? Fear of intimacy? A belief that you are unlovable?

Be ready for love when it does come. Prepare the field and be ready to nourish love. Be loving, and you will be lovable. Be open and receptive to love.

How did you experience love as a child? Did you observe your parents expressing love and affection? Were you raised with lots of hugs? Or in your family, was love expressed through fighting, yelling, crying, door-slamming, manipulation, control, silence, or revenge? If it was, then you'll most likely seek out similar experiences as an adult. You'll find people who will reinforce those ideas. If, as a child, you looked for love and found pain, then as an adult, you'll find pain instead of love... unless you release your old family patterns.

## Exercise: Your Feelings about Love

Answer the following questions as best you can.

- How did your last relationship end?

- How did the one before that end?

- Think about your last two intimate relationships. What were the major issues between you?

- How did these issues remind you of your relationship with one or both of your parents?

Perhaps all of your relationships ended as a result of your partner leaving you. The need in you to be left could stem from a divorce, a parent withdrawing from you because you weren't what they wanted you to be, or a death in the family.

To change the pattern, you need to forgive your parent and understand that you don't have to repeat this old behavior. You free them, and you free yourself.

For every habit or pattern we repeat over and over again, there's a need within us for such repetition. The need corresponds to some belief that we have. If there was no need, we would not have to have it, do it, or be it.

Self-criticism does not break the pattern—letting go of the
need does.

## Exercise: Your Relationships

Answer the following questions as best you can.

- What did you learn about love as a child?

- Did you ever have a boss who was "just like" one of
  your parents? How?

- Is your partner/spouse like one of your parents? How?

- What or whom would you have to forgive in order to
  change this pattern?

- From your new understanding, what would you like
  your relationship to be like?

Your old thoughts and beliefs continue to form your
experiences until you let them go. Your future thoughts
haven't been formed, and you don't know what they'll be.
Your current thought, the one you're thinking right now,
is totally under your control.

We are the only ones who choose our thoughts. We may habitually think the same thought over and over so that it doesn't seem as if we're choosing it. But we did make the original choice. However, we can refuse to think certain thoughts. How often have you refused to think a positive thought about yourself? Well, you can also refuse to think a negative thought about yourself. It just takes practice.

## Exercise: Your Beliefs about Love and Intimacy

Let's examine these beliefs. Answer each of the questions below, then write a positive affirmation (in the present tense) to replace the old belief.

1. **Do I feel worthy of having an intimate relationship?**

   *Sample Answer*: No. Another person would run if they really knew me.

   *Sample Affirmation*: I am lovable and worth knowing.

2. **Am I afraid to love?**

   *Sample Answer*: Yes. I'm afraid that my mate won't be faithful.

   *Sample Affirmation*: I am always secure in love.

3. **What am I "getting" from this belief?**

   *Sample Answer*: I don't let romance into my life.

   *Sample Affirmation*: It is safe for me to open my heart to let love in.

4. **What do I fear will happen if I let go of this belief?**

   *Sample Answer*: I'll be taken advantage of and be hurt.

   *Sample Affirmation*: It is safe for me to share my innermost self with others.

## AFFIRMATIONS FOR LOVE AND INTIMACY

Make these affirmations part of your daily routine. Say them often in the car, at work, while looking in the mirror, or anytime you feel your negative beliefs surfacing.

♦ I love and accept myself, and I am safe.

- Love is eternal.

- Love makes me feel free.

- It is safe for me to be in love.

- My partner and I each take care of ourselves.

- My partner and I are always equal partners.

- Jealousy is only insecurity. I now develop my own self-esteem.

- People love me when I am myself.

- I am worthy of love.

- Loving myself and others gets easier every day.

- The more I open up to love, the safer I am.

- My partner and I respect each other's decisions.

- I now create a long-lasting, loving relationship.

- I give myself permission to experience intimate love.

- All my relationships are harmonious.

# DAY 14

# Creativity

Today our topic is creativity, which we all possess and can develop much more than we might realize.

You can never express yourself creatively by talking or thinking about what a klutz you are. If you say, "I am not creative," then that's an affirmation that will be true for you for as long as you continue to use it. There's an innate creativity flowing through you, and if you let it out, it will surprise and delight you. You're tapped in to the creative flow of energy in the Universe. Some of you may express yourself more creatively than others, but everyone can do it.

We create our lives every day. Each of us has unique talents and abilities. Unfortunately, too many of us had well-meaning adults stifle that creativity when we were children. I had a teacher who once told me I couldn't dance because I was too tall. A friend was told he couldn't draw because he drew the wrong tree. It's all so silly. But we were obedient children and believed the messages. Now we can go beyond them.

Another false assumption is that you must be an artist to be creative. That's just one form of creativity, and there are so many more. You're creating every moment of your life—from the most common, ordinary creation of new cells in your body, to your emotional responses, to your present job, to your bank account, to your relationships with friends, and to your very attitudes about yourself. It's all creativity.

Also, you could be a really good bed-maker, you could cook delicious food, you could do your job creatively, you could be an artist in the garden, or you could be inventive in the ways in which you're kind to others. These are a few of the millions of ways of expressing oneself creatively. No matter which way you choose, you'll want to feel satisfaction and be deeply fulfilled by all that you do.

You're divinely guided by Spirit at all times. Know that Spirit makes no mistakes. When there's a strong desire within you to express or create something, know that this feeling is Divine discontent. Your longing is your calling—and no matter what it is, if you go with it, you'll be guided, guarded, and assured of success. When a purpose or path is laid before you, you have the choice to just trust and let it flow, or remain stuck in fear. Trusting the perfection that resides within you is the key. I know that it can be frightening! Everybody is afraid of something, but you can do it anyway. Remember, the Universe loves you and wants you to succeed at everything you do. You're expressing yourself creatively every moment of every day. You're being you in your own unique way. Knowing that, you can now release any false mental beliefs that you're not creative, and go forward with each and every project that comes to mind.

Never make the mistake of thinking that you're too old for anything. My own life didn't begin to have meaning until I was in my mid–40s, when I started teaching. At age 50, I started my publishing company on a very small scale. At 55, I ventured into the world of computers, taking classes and overcoming my fear of them. At 60, I started my first garden and have become an avid organic gardener who grows her own food. At 70, I enrolled in a children's art class. A few years later, I totally changed my handwriting—I became inspired by author Vimala Rodgers, who wrote *Your Handwriting Can Change Your Life*. At 75, I graduated to an adult art class and have started to sell my paintings. My current art teacher wants me to get involved with sculpture next. And recently, I took up yoga, and my body is making positive changes.

A few months ago, I decided to stretch myself in areas that scared me, and I took up ballroom dancing. Now I'm taking several classes a week, and I'm fulfilling my childhood dream of learning to dance.

I love to learn things I haven't experienced. Who knows what I'll do in the future? What I do know is that I'll be doing my affirmations and expressing new creativity until the day I leave this planet.

If there's a particular project you want to work on, or if you just want to be more creative in general, then you can use some of the following affirmations. Use them joyously as you release your creativity in a million and one different projects.

## AFFIRMATIONS FOR CREATIVITY

Make these affirmations part of your daily routine. Say them often in the car, at work, while looking in the mirror, or anytime you feel your negative beliefs surfacing.

- I release all resistance to expressing my creativity fully.

- I create easily and effortlessly when I let my thoughts come from the loving space of my own heart.

- I do something new or at least different—every day.

- There is ample time and opportunity for creative expression in whatever area I choose.

- My family totally supports me in fulfilling my dreams.

- All of my creative projects bring me great satisfaction.

- I know that I can create miracles in my life.

- I feel good expressing myself in all sorts of creative ways.

- I am my own unique self: special, creative, and wonderful.

- My potential is unlimited.

- I am a joyous, creative expression of life.

- My innate creativity surprises and delights me.

- I am a clear thinker and I express myself with ease.

- I give myself permission to be creatively fulfilled.

- My talents are in demand, and my unique gifts are appreciated by those around me.

~

# DAY 15

# Work

Today we're going to explore the topic of work. Our jobs and the work that we do are a reflection of our own self-worth and our value to the world. On one level, work is an exchange of time and services for money. I like to believe that all forms of business are opportunities for us to bless and prosper each other.

The kind of work we do is important to us because we're unique individuals. We want to feel that we're making a contribution to the world. We need to express our own talents, intelligence, and creative ability.

Finding success in a career is a major problem for many people. However, you can always have a successful job if you simply change the way you think about work. You'll never find work a pleasure if you hate your job or you can't stand your boss. What a terrible affirmation that is. It will be impossible for you to ever attract a great job with that belief system. If you want to enjoy your time at work, then you must change your thinking. I'm a great believer in blessing every person, place, and thing in the workplace with love. Begin with your current job: Affirm that it is merely a stepping-stone to far greater positions.

You're in your current job because of things you believed in the past. You drew it to you by your thinking. Perhaps you learned your attitude toward work from your parents. No matter—you can change your thinking now. So bless with love your boss, your co-workers, the location, the building, the elevators or stairs, the offices, the furniture, and each and every customer. This creates a loving mental atmosphere within you, and the entire environment will respond to it.

Thoughts can be changed, and situations can be changed as well. That boss whom we find intolerable could become our champion. That dead-end position with no hope of advancement may open up to a new career full of possibilities. The co-worker who is so annoying might turn out to be, if not a friend, at least someone who's easier to get along with. The salary that we find insufficient can increase in the twinkle of an eye. We could find a wonderful new job.

There are an infinite number of channels if we can change our thinking. Let's open ourselves up to all the possibilities. We must accept in consciousness that abundance and fulfillment can come from anywhere.

The change may be small at first, such as an additional assignment from your boss in which you could demonstrate your intelligence and creativity. You might find that if you don't treat a co-worker like they're the enemy, a noticeable change in behavior may occur. Whatever the change may be, accept and rejoice in it. You're not alone. You are the change. The Power that created you has given you the power to create your own experiences!

## Exercise: Thinking about Your Work Life

- If you could become anything, what would you be?

- If you could have any job that you wanted, what would it be?

- What would you like to change about your current job?

- What would you change about your employer?

- Do you work in a pleasant environment?

- Whom do you need to forgive the most at work?

## Exercise: Self-worth in Your Job

Let's examine your feelings of self-worth in the area of employment. After answering each of the following questions, write an affirmation (in the present tense).

1. **Do I feel worthy of having a good job?**

   *Sample Answer*: Sometimes I don't feel good enough.

   *Sample Affirmation*: I am totally adequate for all situations.

2.  **What do I fear most about work?**

    *Sample Answer*: My employer will find out that I'm no good, will fire me, and I won't find another job.

    *Sample Affirmation*: I center myself in safety and accept the perfection of my life. All is well.

3.  **What am I "getting" from this belief?**

    *Sample Answer*: I people-please at work, and turn my employer into a parent.

    *Sample Affirmation*: It is my mind that creates my experiences. I am unlimited in my ability to create the good in my life.

4.  **What do I fear will happen if I let go of this belief?**

    *Sample Answer*: I would have to grow up and be responsible.

    *Sample Affirmation*: I know that I am worthwhile. It is safe for me to succeed. Life loves me.

## Exercise: Visualization

What would the perfect job be? Take a moment to see yourself in the job. Visualize yourself in the environment, see your co-workers, and feel what it would be like to do work that's completely fulfilling—while you earn a good salary. Hold that vision for yourself, and know that it has been fulfilled in consciousness.

---

Please don't believe that it's hard to get a job. That may be true for many, but it doesn't have to be true for you. You only need one job, and your consciousness will then open the pathway for you. Don't have faith in fear. When you hear of negative trends in business or in the economy, immediately affirm: "It may be true for some, but it is not true for me. I always prosper no matter where I am or what is going on."

You know that you're successful in all that you do. You're inspired and productive. You serve others willingly and gladly. Divine harmony reigns supreme within and around you and within and around each and every person in your workplace.

If you like your job but feel that you're not getting paid enough, then bless your current salary with love. Expressing gratitude for what you have now enables your income to grow. And please, absolutely no more complaining about the job or your co-workers. Your consciousness put you where you are now. Your changing consciousness can lift to you a better position. You can do it!

## Affirmations for Work

Make these affirmations part of your daily routine. Say them often in the car, at work, while looking in the mirror, or anytime you feel your negative beliefs surfacing.

- I deserve to have a successful career, and I accept it now.

- ◆ I enjoy the work I do and the people I work with.

- ◆ I am always relaxed at work.

- ◆ When I encounter problems on the job, I am willing to ask for help.

- ◆ The joy I find in my career is reflected in my overall happiness.

- ◆ My work is recognized by everyone.

- ◆ I am grateful for this employment.

- ◆ I turn every experience into an opportunity.

- ◆ All my supervisors treat me with love and respect.

- ◆ I am capable, competent, and in the perfect place.

- ◆ I see the best in everyone, and they respond in kind.

- ◆ My thoughts create a wonderful new opportunity.

- ◆ Everything I touch is a success.

- ◆ New doors are opening all the time.

- ◆ I am open and receptive to new avenues of income.

# DAY 16

# Money and Prosperity

Today we're going to look at money and prosperity.

You can never create prosperity by talking or thinking about your lack of money. This is wasted thinking and cannot bring you abundance. Dwelling on lack only creates more lack. Poverty thinking brings more poverty. Gratitude thinking brings abundance.

There are a few negative affirmations and attitudes that are guaranteed to keep prosperity beyond your reach—for example: "I never have enough money!" That's a terrible affirmation to use. Another unproductive one is: "Money goes out faster than it comes in." This is poverty thinking of the worst kind. The Universe can only respond to what you believe about yourself and your life. Examine whatever negative thoughts you have about money, and then decide to release them and let them go. They haven't served you well in the past and will not serve you well in the future.

Sometimes people think that their financial problems will be solved by inheriting money from a long-lost relative or winning the lottery. Sure, you can fantasize about such things, or even buy an occasional lottery ticket for fun, but please don't put a lot of attention on acquiring money in this way. This is scarcity thinking, or poverty thinking, and it won't bring lasting good into your life. Affirming, declaring, deserving, and allowing are the steps to demonstrating riches far greater that you could ever win in a lottery.

Another thing that can keep you from prospering is being dishonest. Whatever you give out comes back to you. Always. If you take from life, then life will take from you. It's that simple. You may feel that you don't steal, but are you counting the paper clips and stamps you're taking home from the office? Or are you a person who steals time or robs others of respect—or perhaps steals relationships? All these things count and are a way of saying to the Universe: "I don't really deserve the good in life. I have to sneak it and take it."

Become aware of the beliefs that may be blocking the flow of money in your life. Then change those beliefs and begin to create new, abundant thinking. Even if no one else in your family has done this, you can open your mind to the concept of money flowing into your life.

If you want to prosper, then you must use prosperity thinking. There are two prosperity affirmations that I've used for many years, and they work well for me. They'll also work for you. They are:

"My income is constantly increasing," and "I prosper wherever I turn."

I had very little money when I started using these affirmations, but consistent practice has made them come true for me.

As I've said many times, your prosperity consciousness is not dependent upon money; your flow of money is dependent upon your prosperity consciousness.

Our pursuit of money must contribute to the quality of our lives. If it doesn't—that is, if we hate what we do in order to make money, then money will be useless. Prosperity involves the quality of our lives, as well as any amount of money that we possess.

Prosperity is not defined by money alone; it encompasses time, love, success, joy, comfort, beauty, and wisdom. For example, you can be poor with respect to time. If you feel rushed, pressured, and harried, then your time is steeped in poverty. But if you feel you have all the time you need to finish any task at hand, and you're confident that you can finish any job, then you're prosperous when it comes to time.

Or what about success? Do you feel that it's beyond your reach and completely unattainable? Or do you feel that you can be a success in your own right? If you do, then you're rich with respect to success.

Know that whatever your beliefs are, they can be changed in this moment. The power that created you has given you the power to create your own experiences. You can change!

## Exercise: Mirror Work

Stand up with your arms outstretched, and say, "I am open and receptive to all good." How does that feel?

Now, look into the mirror and say it again with feeling.

What kinds of emotions come up for you? It feels liberating, doesn't it? Do this exercise every morning. It's a wonderfully symbolic gesture that may increase your prosperity consciousness and bring more good into your life.

## Exercise: Your Feelings about Money

Let's examine your feelings of self-worth in this area. Answer the following questions as best you can.

- Go back to the mirror. Look into your eyes and say, "My biggest fear about money is..." Write down your answer and tell yourself why you feel that way.

- What did you learn about money as a child?

- Did your parents grow up during an economic downturn? What were their thoughts about money?

- How were finances handled in your family?

- How do you handle money now?

- What would you like to change about your money consciousness?

## Exercise: Your Money Consciousness

Let's further examine your feelings of self-worth in the money area. Answer the following questions as best you can. After each negative belief, create a positive affirmation in the present tense to take its place.

1.  **Do I feel worthy of having and enjoying money?**

    *Sample Answer*: Not really. I spend money as soon as I get it.

    *Sample Affirmation*: I bless the money I have. It is safe to save money and let my money work for me.

2.  **What is my greatest fear regarding money?**

    *Sample Answer*: I'm afraid that I'll always be broke.

    *Sample Affirmation*: I now accept limitless abundance from a limitless Universe.

3.  **What am I "getting" from this belief?**

    *Sample Answer*: I get to stay poor, and I get to be taken care of by others.

    *Sample Affirmation*: I claim my own power and lovingly create my own reality. I trust the process of life.

4.  **What do I fear will happen to me if I let go of this belief?**

    *Sample Answer*: No one will love me and take care of me.

    *Sample Affirmation*: I am safe in the Universe, and all life loves and supports me.

## AFFIRMATIONS FOR MONEY AND PROSPERITY

Make these affirmations part of your daily routine. Say them often in the car, at work, while looking in the mirror, or anytime you feel your negative beliefs surfacing.

- I live in a loving, abundant, harmonious Universe, and I am grateful.

- I am a magnet for money. Prosperity of every kind is drawn to me.

- I am worthy of having money in the bank.

- My income is constantly increasing.

- Today money comes to me in expected and unexpected ways.

- My credit rating is getting better all the time.

- I spend money wisely.

- I always have as much as I need.

- I have as much money as I can accept.

- I bless all of my bills with love. I pay them on time.

- I am always financially solvent.

- I am joyfully providing for my retirement.

- I enjoy saving, and I spend in balance.

- I delight in the financial security that is a constant in my life.

- I give myself permission to prosper.

~

# DAY 17

# Addictions

Addictive behavior, which is another way of saying "I'm not good enough," is our topic for today. When we're caught in this type of behavior, we're trying to run away from ourselves. We don't want to be in touch with our feelings. Something that we're believing, remembering, saying, or doing is too painful for us to look at; so we overeat, drink, engage in compulsive sexual behavior, take pills, spend money that we don't have, and attract abusive love relationships.

There are 12-step programs that deal with most of these addictions, and they work well for thousands of people. If you have a serious addiction problem,

I encourage you to attend Alcoholics Anonymous (AA) or Al-Anon meetings. They will provide you with the help you need as you go through these important changes.

In this chapter, we can't hope to duplicate the results that these programs have produced for people with addictive behavior. I believe that we must first realize that there's a need in ourselves for these compulsive actions. That need must be released before the behavior can be changed.

Loving and approving of yourself, trusting in the process of life, and feeling safe because you know the power of your own mind are extremely important issues when dealing with addictive behaviors. My experience with addicted persons has shown me that most of these individuals possess a deep self-hatred. They're very unforgiving of themselves. Day after day, they punish themselves. Why? Because somewhere along the line (most likely when they were children), they bought into the idea that they weren't good enough—they were "bad" and in need of punishment.

Early childhood experiences that involve physical, emotional, or sexual abuse contribute to that type of self-hatred. Honesty, forgiveness, self-love, and a willingness to live in the truth can help heal these early wounds and give addictive individuals a reprieve from their behavior. I also find the addictive personality to be a fearful one. There's a great fear of letting go and trusting the process of life. As long as we believe that the world is an unsafe place with people and situations waiting to "get" us—then that belief will be our reality.

Are you willing to let go of ideas and beliefs that don't support and nurture you? If so, then you're ready to continue this journey.

## Exercise: Release Your Addictions

This is where the changes take place—right here and now in your own mind! Take some deep breaths; close your eyes; and think about the person, place, or thing that you're addicted to. Think of the confusion behind the addiction. You're trying to fix what you think is wrong inside of you by grabbing on to something that's outside of you. The point of power is in the present moment, and you can begin to make a shift today.

Once again, be willing to release the need. Say: "I am willing to release the need for… in my life. I release it now and trust in the process of life to meet my needs."

Say this statement every morning in your daily meditation and prayers. You've taken another step toward freedom.

## Exercise: Your Secret Addiction

List 10 secrets you've never shared with anyone regarding your addiction. If you're an overeater, maybe you've eaten out of a garbage can. If you're an alcoholic, you may have kept alcohol in your car so you could drink while driving. If you're a compulsive gambler, perhaps you put your family in jeopardy in order to borrow money to feed your gambling problem. Be totally honest and open.

How do you feel now? Look at your "worst" secret. Visualize yourself at that period in your life, and love that person. Express how much you love and forgive him or her. Look into the mirror and say: "I forgive you, and I love you exactly as you are." Breathe.

## Exercise: Ask Your Family

Let's go back to your childhood for a moment and answer a few questions. Write down the answers and reflect on them.

- My mother always made me…

- What I really wanted her to say was…

- What my mother really didn't know was…

- My father told me I shouldn't…

- If my father only knew…

- I wish I could have told my father…

- Mother, I forgive you for…

- Father, I forgive you for…

## AFFIRMATIONS FOR ADDICTIONS

Make these affirmations part of your daily routine. Say them often in the car, at work, while looking in the mirror, or anytime you feel your negative beliefs surfacing.

- I am at peace.

- I am totally adequate for all situations.

- I release my stress with deep breathing.

- I have the power, strength, and knowledge to handle everything in my life.

- I nourish myself with my own love.

- I radiate acceptance, and I am deeply loved by others.

- I release the need to be perfect. I am enough just as I am.

- I am open to the wisdom within.

- I see my patterns and make changes without embarrassment and guilt.

- I recognize that awareness is the first step in healing or changing. I become more aware each day.

- I relax into the flow of life and let life provide all that I need easily and comfortably.

- I am willing to create new thoughts about myself and my life.

- No one can mistreat me. I love, appreciate, and respect myself.

- I am gentle and kind with myself as I grow and change.

- No person, place, or thing has any power over me. I am free.

~

# DAY 18

# Aging

Today we're going to explore a subject that many of us don't like to think about—aging. The fact is that no matter what age we are, we will all grow older. However, we will also have great control over how we shall age.

What are the things that age us? Certain beliefs about aging, such as the belief that we have to get sick when we get old. The belief in dis-ease. Hating the body. Believing in a lack of time. Anger and hatred. Self-hatred. Bitterness. Shame and guilt. Fear. Prejudice. Self-righteousness. Being judgmental. Carrying burdens. Giving up our control to others. These are all beliefs that age us.

We don't have to accept these negative concepts. We can turn all of this around. It doesn't have to continue to be this way. We can take our power back.

Feeling vital and energetic is much more important than a facial line or two (or even more), yet we've agreed that unless we're young and beautiful, we're not acceptable. Why would we agree to such a belief? Where did we lose our love and compassion for ourselves and for each other? We've made living in our bodies an uncomfortable experience. Each day we look for something that's wrong with us, and we worry about every wrinkle. This only makes us feel bad and creates more wrinkles. This isn't self-love. This is self-hatred, and it only contributes to our lack of self-esteem.

We used to live very short lives—first only till our mid-teens, then our 20s, then our 30s, then our 40s. Even at the turn of the century, it was considered old to be 50. In 1900, our life expectancy was 47 years. Now we're accepting 80 as a normal life span. Why can't we take a quantum leap in consciousness and make the new level of acceptance 120 or 150 years?!

It's not out of our reach. I see living much longer becoming normal and natural for most of us in a generation or two. Forty-five used to be middle-aged, but that won't be true anymore. I see 75 becoming the new middle age. For generations, we've allowed the numbers that correspond to how many years we've been on the planet tell us how to feel and how to behave. As with any other aspect of life, what we mentally accept and believe about aging becomes true for us. Well, it's time to change our beliefs about aging! When I look around and see frail, sick, frightened older people, I say to myself, "It doesn't have to be that way." Many of us have learned that by changing our thinking, we can change our lives.

I know we can change our beliefs about aging and make the aging process a positive, vibrant, healthy experience. But in order to do so, we "Elders of Excellence" need to get out of the victim mentality. It's time for our elders to take back their power from the medical and pharmaceutical industries. They're being buffeted about by high-tech medicine, which is very expensive and destroys their health. It's time for all of us (and especially the elders) to learn to take control of our own health. We need to learn about the body-mind connection—to know that what we do, say, and think contributes to either dis-ease or vibrant health.

## Exercise: Your Beliefs about Aging

Answer the following questions as best you can.

- How are your parents aging? (Or how did they age if they've passed away?)

- How old do you feel?

- What are you doing to help our society/country/ planet?

- How do you create love in your life?

- Who are your positive role models?

- What are you teaching your children about aging?

- What are you doing today to prepare for healthy, happy, and vital elder years?

- How do you feel about and treat older people now?

- How do you envision your life when you're 60, 75, 85?

- How do you want to be treated when you're older?

- How do you want to die?

Now go back and mentally turn each negative answer above into a positive affirmation. Envision your later years as your treasure years.

―――――――――――――

There's a pot of gold at the end of this rainbow. We know the treasures are there. The later years of our life are to be the years of our greatest treasures. We must learn how to make these the best years of our lives. We learn these secrets later in life, and they are to be shared with the generations coming up. I know that what I call "youthening" can be done; it's just a matter of finding out how.

Here are some of the secrets of youthening, as far as I'm concerned:

- Release the word "old" from our vocabulary.

- Turn "aging" into "living longer."

- Be willing to accept new concepts.

- Take a quantum leap in thinking.

- Modify our beliefs.

- Reject manipulation.

- Change what we consider "normal."

- Turn dis-ease into vibrant health.

- Take good care of our bodies.

- Release limiting beliefs.

- Be willing to adapt our thinking.

- Embrace new ideas.

- Accept the truth about ourselves.

- Give selfless service to our communities.

We want to create a conscious ideal of our later years as the most rewarding phase of our lives. We need to know that our future is always bright no matter what our age. We can do this if we just change our thoughts. It's time to dispel the fearful images of old age. It's time to take a quantum leap in our thinking. We need to take the word "old" out of our vocabulary and become a world where the long-lived are still young—and where life expectancy isn't given a finite number. We want to see our later years become our treasure years.

## AFFIRMATIONS FOR AGING

Make these affirmations part of your daily routine. Say them often in the car, at work, while looking in the mirror, or anytime you feel your negative beliefs surfacing.

- ◆ I release all age-related fears.

- ◆ I am beautiful in mind and body.

- ◆ I am self-sufficient and strong.

- ◆ It is my birthright to live fully and freely.

- I love and am loved by everyone in my world.

- I have vibrant health no matter what age I am.

- My joyful thoughts create my joyful world.

- Each moment in life is perfect.

- People appreciate me at every age.

- I rise above all limitations. I am Divinely guided and inspired.

- I am surrounded by wonderful people throughout my life.

- I am beautiful and empowered at every age.

- My life continues to get better and better.

- I radiate health, happiness, prosperity, and peace of mind.

- I am always the perfect age for where I am in my life.

~

# DAY 19

# Stress-free Living

Today we'll explore how to make life as stress-free as possible.

This is the moment in which you're either enjoying or not enjoying your life. What you're thinking is creating the way you feel in your body right now, and it's also creating your experiences of tomorrow. If you're stressing out over every little thing and making mountains out of molehills, you'll never find inner peace.

We talk a lot about stress these days. Everyone seems to be stressed out by something. Stress seems to be a buzzword, and we use it to the point where I think it's a cop-out: "I'm so stressed," or "This is so stressful," or "All this stress, stress, stress."

I think that stress is a fearful reaction to life's constant changes. It's an excuse we often use for not taking responsibility for our feelings. If we can put the blame out there on someone or something, then we can just play the innocent victim. Being the victim doesn't make us feel good, and it doesn't change the situation.

Often we're stressing ourselves out because we have our priorities mixed up. So many of us feel that money is the most important thing in our lives. This is simply not true. There's something far more important and precious to us— without which we couldn't live. What is that? It's our breath.

Our breath is the most precious substance in our lives, and yet we totally take it for granted that when we exhale, our next breath will be there. If we didn't take another breath, we wouldn't last three minutes. Now if the Power that created us has given us enough breath to last as long as we shall live, can't we have faith that everything else we need will also be supplied?

When we trust life to take care of all our little problems, then stress just melts away.

You don't have time to waste on negative thinking or emotions, because that only creates more of what you say you don't want. If you're doing some positive affirmations and you're not getting the results you desire, then check to see how often during the day you allow yourself to feel bad or upset. These emotions are probably just the thing that's frustrating you, delaying the manifestation of your affirmations, and stopping the flow of your good.

The next time you realize how stressed you are, ask yourself what's scaring you. Stress is just fear, it's that simple. You don't need to be afraid of life or your own emotions. Find out what you're doing to yourself that's creating this fear within you. Your inner goal is joy, harmony, and peace. Harmony is being at peace with yourself. It's not possible to have stress and inner harmony at the same time. When you're at peace, you do one thing at a time. You don't let things get to you.

So when you feel stressed, do something to release the fear: Breathe deeply or go for a brisk walk. Affirm to yourself:

*"I am the only power in my world; and I create a peaceful, loving, joyful, fulfilling life."*

You want to move through life feeling safe. Don't give a little word like "stress" a lot of power. Don't use it as an excuse for creating tension in your body. Nothing— no person, place, or thing—has any power over you. You're the only thinker in your mind, and your thoughts are the ones that create your life.

So train yourself to think thoughts that make you feel good. That way you'll always be creating your life out of joy and in joy. Joy always brings more to be joyous about.

## Affirmations for
## Stress-free Living

Make these affirmations part of your daily routine. Say them often in the car, at work, while looking in the mirror, or anytime you feel your negative beliefs surfacing.

- I let go of all fear and doubt, and life becomes simple and easy for me.

- I create a stress-free world for myself.

- I relax all of my neck muscles, and I let go of any tension in my shoulders.

- I slowly breathe in and out, and I find myself relaxing more and more with each breath.

- I am a capable person and I can handle anything that comes my way.

- I am centered and focused. I feel more secure each day.

- I am even-tempered and emotionally well balanced.

- I am at ease with myself, and I am at ease with other people.

- I am safe when I express my feelings. I can be serene in any situation.

- I have a wonderful relationship with my friends, family members, and co-workers. I am appreciated.

- I am comfortable with my finances. I am always able to pay my bills on time.

- I trust myself to deal with any problems that arise during the day.

- I let go of all negativity that rests in my body and mind.

- I am in the process of making positive changes in all areas of my life.

- I have the strength to remain calm in the face of change.

~

# DAY 20

# Practicing Your Affirmations

Like any other new thing you're learning, it takes practice to make affirmations part of your life. The process of learning is always the same no matter what the subject—whether you're learning to drive a car, or type, or play tennis, or think in a positive manner. First, we fumble and bumble as our subconscious mind learns by trial, and yet, every time we come back to our practicing, it gets easier, and we do it a little better. Of course, you won't be "perfect" the first day. You will be doing whatever you can do. That's good enough for a start.

Say to yourself often, "I'm doing the best I can."

I well remember my first lecture. When I came down from the podium, I immediately said to myself, "Louise, you were wonderful. You were absolutely fantastic for the first time. When you have done five or six of these, you will be a pro."

A couple of hours later, I said to myself, "I think we could change a few things. Let's adjust this, and let's adjust that." I refused to criticize myself in any way.

If I had come off the podium and begun berating myself with, "Oh, you were so awful. You made this mistake, and you made that mistake," then I would have dreaded my second lecture. As it was, the second one was better than the first, and by the sixth one, I was feeling like a pro.

## Exercise: Daily Affirmations

Take one or two affirmations and write them 10 or 20 times a day. Read them aloud with enthusiasm. Make a song out of your affirmations and sing them with joy. Let your mind go over these affirmations all day long.

Affirmations that are used consistently become beliefs and will always produce results, sometimes in ways that we cannot even imagine.

## Exercise: Claim the New

Visualize or imagine yourself having or doing or being what you are working toward. Fill in all the details. Feel, see, taste, touch, hear. Notice other people's reactions to your new state. Make it all okay with you no matter what their reactions are.

## Exercise:
## Expand Your Knowledge

Read everything you can to expand your awareness and understanding of how the mind works. There is so much knowledge out there for you. This book is only one step on your pathway! Get other viewpoints. Hear other people say it in a different way. Study with a group for a while until you go beyond them.

---

This is a life work. The more you learn, the more you know, the more you practice and apply, the better you get to feel, and the more wonderful your life will be. Doing this work makes you feel good!

Love who and what you are and what you do. Laugh at yourself and at life, and nothing can touch you. It's all temporary anyway. Next lifetime you will do it differently anyway, so why not do it differently right now?

When you go to bed at night, close your eyes and again be thankful for all the good in your life. It will bring more good in.

Please do not listen to the news or watch it on TV the last thing at night. The news is only a list of disasters, and you don't want to take that into your dream state. Much clearing work is done in the dream state, and you can ask your dreams for help with anything you are working on. You will often find an answer by morning.

Go to sleep peacefully. Trust the process of life to be on your side and take care of everything for your highest good and greatest joy.

There is no need to make drudgery out of what you are doing. It can be fun. It can be a game. It can be a joy. It's up to you! Even practicing forgiveness and releasing resentment can be fun, if you want to make it so. Again, make up a little song about that person or situation that is so hard to release. When you sing a ditty, it lightens up the whole procedure. When I work with clients privately, I bring laughter into the procedure as soon as I can. The quicker we can laugh about the whole thing, the easier it is to let it go.

If you saw your problems on a stage in a play by Neil Simon, you would laugh yourself right out of the chair. Tragedy and comedy are the same thing. It just depends on your viewpoint! "Oh, what fools we mortals be."

Do whatever you can to make your transformational change a joy and a pleasure. Have fun!

# DAY 21

# The Way Forward

How often have you lamented about what you didn't want? Did it ever bring you what you really wanted? Fighting the negative is a total waste of time if you really want to make changes in your life. The more you dwell on what you don't want, the more of it you create.

"I don't want to be fat." "I don't want to be broke." "I don't want to be old." "I don't want to live here." "I don't want to have this relationship." "I don't want to be like my mother/father." "I don't want to be stuck in this job." "I don't want to have this hair/nose/body." "I don't want to be lonely." "I don't want to be unhappy." "I don't want to be sick."

Such self-criticism is just the mind retaining old beliefs. It shows how we're culturally taught to fight the negative mentally—thinking that if we do so, the positive will automatically come to us. It doesn't work that way.

In the days when my own self-denial was so prevalent, I would occasionally slap my own face. I didn't know the meaning of self-acceptance. My belief in my own lacks and limitations was stronger than anything anyone else could say to the contrary. If someone told me I was loved, my immediate reaction was, "Why? What could anyone possibly see in me?" Or the classic thought, "If they only knew what I was really like inside, they wouldn't love me."

I was not aware that all good begins with accepting that which is within one's self, and loving that self which is you. It took quite a while to develop a peaceful, loving relationship with myself.

First, I used to hunt for the little things about myself that I thought were "good qualities." Even this helped, and my own health began to improve. Good health begins with loving the self. So do prosperity and love and creative self-expression. Later I learned to love and approve of all of me, even those qualities I thought were "not good enough." That was when I really began to make progress.

Think for a moment of a tomato plant. A healthy plant can have over a hundred tomatoes on it. In order to get this tomato plant with all these tomatoes on it, we need to start with a small dried seed. That seed doesn't look like a tomato plant. It sure doesn't taste like a tomato plant. If you didn't know for sure, you would not even believe it could be a tomato plant. However, let's say you plant this seed in fertile soil, and you water it and let the sun shine on it.

When the first little, tiny shoot comes up, you don't stomp on it and say, "That's not a tomato plant." Rather, you look at it and say, "Oh boy! Here it comes," and you watch it grow with delight. In time, if you continue to water it and give it lots of sunshine and pull away any weeds, you might have a tomato plant with more than a hundred luscious tomatoes. It all began with that one tiny seed.

It is the same with creating a new experience for yourself. The soil you plant in is your subconscious mind. The seed is the new affirmation. The whole new experience is in this tiny seed. You water it with affirmations. You let the sunshine of positive thoughts beam on it. You weed the garden by pulling out the negative thoughts that come up. And when you first see the tiniest little evidence, you don't stomp on it and say, "That's not enough!" Instead, you look at this first breakthrough and exclaim with glee, "Oh boy! Here it comes! It's working!"

As we learn to use affirmations, we may also be drawn to adopt a more holistic approach to living. The holistic philosophy is to nurture and nourish the entire being—the body, the mind, and the spirit. If we ignore any of these areas, we are incomplete; we lack wholeness. It doesn't matter where we start as long as we also include the other areas.

If we begin with the body, we would want to work with nutrition, to learn the relationship between our choice of food and beverages, and how they affect the way we feel. We want to make the best choices for our body. There are herbs and vitamins, homeopathy, and Bach Flower Remedies. We might explore colonics.

We would want to find a form of exercise that appeals to us. Exercise is something that strengthens our bones and keeps our bodies young. In addition to sports and swimming, consider dancing, Tai-Chi, martial arts, and yoga. I love my trampoline and use it daily. My slant board enhances my periods of relaxation.

We might want to explore some form of bodywork such as Rolfing, Hellerwork or Trager. Massage, foot reflexology, acupuncture, or chiropractic work are all beneficial, as well. There is also the Alexander technique, Bioenergetics, the Feldenkrais Method, Touch for Health, and Reiki forms of bodywork.

With the mind, there are lots of psychological techniques: Gestalt, hypnosis, rebirthing, psychodrama, past-life regressions, art therapy, and even dream work. Meditation in any of its forms is a wonderful way to quiet the mind and allow your own "knowingness" to come to the surface. I usually just sit with my eyes closed and say, "What is it I need to know?" and then

I wait quietly for an answer. If the answer comes, fine; if it doesn't, fine. It will come another day.

In the Spiritual Realm, there is prayer, there is meditation, and becoming connected with your Higher Source. For me, practicing forgiveness and unconditional love are spiritual practices.

There are many spiritual groups. In addition to the Christian churches, there are metaphysical churches, such as Religious Science and Unity. There is the Self-Realization Fellowship, M.S.I.A., Transcendental Meditation, the Siddha Foundation, and so on.

So let's now recap the ways you can reinforce your new learning and move forward. I suggest:

- writing affirmations

- saying affirmations aloud

- singing affirmations

- expressing gratitude

- taking time for relaxation exercises

- sitting in meditation or prayer

- enjoying exercise

- practicing good nutrition

- using visualization and mental imagery

- reading and study

By practicing as many of these methods as you can, you will begin to demonstrate your results of this work. You will see the little miracles occur in your life. The things you are ready to eliminate will go of their own accord. The things and events you want will pop up in your life seemingly out of the blue. You will get bonuses you never imagined!

# Afterword

We've now explored using affirmations in many different areas of life. The previous chapters show you the many diverse ways that you can use and create positive affirmations for yourself.

This book can send you on the positive pathway to a wonderful life. However, you must use it. Words sitting in a book will do nothing to improve the quality of your life.

Make affirmations part of your life. Put different affirmations in different parts of your home. You might have an affirmation you keep at the office for work issues. If you don't want others to see it, then put it in your desk drawer so only you see it.

A car affirmation for safe and peaceful driving might be on your dashboard. (Hint, hint… if you're always cursing at other drivers, then all the poor drivers will automatically be attracted to you. They'll be fulfilling your affirmation.)

Cursing is an affirmation, worrying is an affirmation, and hatred is an affirmation. All of these are attracting to you that which you're affirming. Love, appreciation, gratitude, and compliments are also affirmations and will similarly attract to you that which you're affirming.

Just as it doesn't matter where you begin cleaning the house, it also doesn't matter which area of your life you begin to change first. It's best to start with something simple because you'll get results quickly and therefore develop confidence to tackle the larger issues.

Once you've done your affirmations, then it's time to release them and let them go. You've decided what you want. You've affirmed them in both thought and word. Now you must release them to the Universe so that the laws of life can bring them to you.

If you worry and fret about how your affirmations will come true, you're just delaying the whole process. It's not your job to figure out how to bring your affirmations to fruition. The way the Laws of Attraction work, you declare that you have something, and then the Universe brings it to you. The Universe is far cleverer than you are and knows every possible way to make your affirmations come true. The only reason for delay and for seemingly denying you is that there's a part of you that doesn't believe that you deserve it. Or perhaps your beliefs are so strong that they overpower your affirmations.

Remember...

No matter how wonderful the present moment is, the future can be even more fulfilling and joyous. The Universe always waits in smiling repose for us to align our thinking with its laws. When we are in alignment, everything flows.

It *is* possible. If I can do it, you can do it. We all can do it. Make the effort—you will be so pleased. Your whole world will change for the better. You'll be so happy about the positive changes that are happening in your life.

*This will be the start of a new you!*

# About the Author

**Louise Hay** was an inspirational teacher who educated millions since the 1984 publication of her best-seller *You Can Heal Your Life*, which has more than 50 million copies in print worldwide. Renowned for demonstrating the power of affirmations to bring about positive change, Louise was the author of more than 30 books for adults and children, including the best-sellers *The Power Is Within You* and *Heal Your Body*. In addition to her books, Louise produced numerous audio and video programs, card decks, online courses, and other resources for leading a healthy, joyous, and fulfilling life.

**www.louisehay.com**
**www.healyourlife.com**
**www.facebook.com/louiselhay**

# Also by Louise Hay

## BOOKS

All Is Well (with Mona Lisa Schulz, M.D., Ph.D.)

The Bone Broth Secret (with Heather Dane)

Colors & Numbers

Embrace Your Power

Experience Your Good Now!

Heal Your Body (also available in Spanish)

Heal Your Mind (with Mona Lisa Schulz, M.D., Ph.D.)

Heart Thoughts

I Can Do It® (book-with-download)

I Think, I Am! (children's book with Kristina Tracy)

Life Loves You (with Robert Holden)

Love Your Body

Love Yourself, Heal Your Life Workbook

Meditations to Heal Your Life (also available in Spanish)

Mirror Work

The Power Is Within You (also available in Spanish)

Trust Life

You Can Create an Exceptional Life (with Cheryl Richardson, also available in Spanish)

You Can Heal Your Heart (with David Kessler)

You Can Heal Your Life (also available in a gift edition and in Spanish)

You Can Heal Your Life Companion Book

## AUDIO PROGRAMS

All Is Well (audiobook)

Anger Releasing

Cancer

Change and Transition

Dissolving Barriers

Embracing Change

Evening Meditation

Feeling Fine Affirmations

Forgiveness/Loving the Inner Child

Heal Your Mind (audiobook)

How to Love Yourself (audiobook)

I Can Do It® (audiobook)

Life Loves You (audiobook)

Love Your Body (audiobook)

Meditations for Loving Yourself to Great Health

Meditations for Personal Healing

Morning and Evening Meditations

101 Power Thoughts

Overcoming Fears (audiobook)

The Power Is Within You (audiobook)

The Power of Your Spoken Word

Receiving Prosperity

Self-Esteem Affirmations (subliminal)

Self-Healing

Stress-Free (subliminal)

Subliminal Affirmations for Positive Self-Esteem

Totality of Possibilities

What I Believe and Deep Relaxation

You Can Heal Your Heart (audiobook)

You Can Heal Your Life (audiobook)

You Can Heal Your Life Study Course

## VIDEOS

Dissolving Barriers

Doors Opening

Painting the Future: Tales of Everyday Magic

Receiving Prosperity

You Can Heal Your Life Study Course (DVD)

You Can Heal Your Life, The Movie (available in standard and expanded editions)

You Can Trust Your Life (with Cheryl Richardson)

## INSPIRATIONAL CARDS

Heart Thoughts Cards (mobile app)

How to Love Yourself Cards (mobile app and deck)

I Can Do It® Cards (mobile app)

Life Loves You Cards (mobile app and deck with Robert Holden)

Power Thought Cards (mobile app and deck)

## JOURNAL

The Gift of Gratitude: A Guided Journal for Counting Your Blessings

## CALENDAR

I Can Do It® Calendar (for each individual year)

## ONLINE COURSES

Loving Yourself: 21 Days to Improved Self-Esteem with Mirror Work (with Robert Holden)

You Can Trust Your Life: Create Your Best Year Yet (with Cheryl Richardson)

All of the above are available at your local bookstore, or may be ordered by visiting:

Hay House UK: www.hayhouse.co.uk
Hay House USA: www.hayhouse.com®
Hay House Australia: www.hayhouse.com.au
Hay House India: www.hayhouse.co.in

We hope you enjoyed this Hay House book. If you'd like to receive our online catalog featuring additional information on Hay House books and products, or if you'd like to find out more about the Hay Foundation, please contact:

Hay House, Inc., P.O. Box 5100, Carlsbad, CA 92018-5100
(760) 431-7695 or (800) 654-5126
(760) 431-6948 (fax) or (800) 650-5115 (fax)
www.hayhouse.com® • www.hayfoundation.org

———

*Published in Australia by:* Hay House Australia Pty. Ltd.,
18/36 Ralph St., Alexandria NSW 2015
*Phone:* 612-9669-4299 • *Fax:* 612-9669-4144
www.hayhouse.com.au

*Published in the United Kingdom by:* Hay House UK, Ltd.,
The Sixth Floor, Watson House, 54 Baker Street, London W1U 7BU
*Phone:* +44 (0)20 3927 7290 • *Fax:* +44 (0)20 3927 7291
www.hayhouse.co.uk

*Published in India by:* Hay House Publishers India,
Muskaan Complex, Plot No. 3, B-2, Vasant Kunj, New Delhi 110 070
*Phone:* 91-11-4176-1620 • *Fax:* 91-11-4176-1630
www.hayhouse.co.in

———

Access New Knowledge.
Anytime. Anywhere.

Learn and evolve at your own pace
with the world's leading experts.

www.hayhouseU.com

## CONNECT WITH
# HAY HOUSE
## ONLINE

🌐 hayhouse.co.uk          **f** @hayhouse

📷 @hayhouseuk            🐦 @hayhouseuk

▶ @hayhouseuk            ♪ @hayhouseuk

*Find out all about our latest books & card decks • Be the first to know about exclusive discounts • Interact with our authors in live broadcasts • Celebrate the cycle of the seasons with us • Watch free videos from your favourite authors • Connect with like-minded souls*

'*The gateways to wisdom and knowledge are always open.*'

**Louise Hay**